C-329   CAREER EXAMINATION SERIES

This is your
PASSBOOK for...

Heating Plant Technician

Test Preparation Study Guide
Questions & Answers

COPYRIGHT NOTICE

This book is SOLELY intended for, is sold ONLY to, and its use is RESTRICTED to individual, bona fide applicants or candidates who qualify by virtue of having seriously filed applications for appropriate license, certificate, professional and/or promotional advancement, higher school matriculation, scholarship, or other legitimate requirements of education and/or governmental authorities.

This book is NOT intended for use, class instruction, tutoring, training, duplication, copying, reprinting, excerption, or adaptation, etc., by:

1) Other publishers
2) Proprietors and/or Instructors of "Coaching" and/or Preparatory Courses
3) Personnel and/or Training Divisions of commercial, industrial, and governmental organizations
4) Schools, colleges, or universities and/or their departments and staffs, including teachers and other personnel
5) Testing Agencies or Bureaus
6) Study groups which seek by the purchase of a single volume to copy and/or duplicate and/or adapt this material for use by the group as a whole without having purchased individual volumes for each of the members of the group
7) Et al.

Such persons would be in violation of appropriate Federal and State statutes.

PROVISION OF LICENSING AGREEMENTS – Recognized educational, commercial, industrial, and governmental institutions and organizations, and others legitimately engaged in educational pursuits, including training, testing, and measurement activities, may address request for a licensing agreement to the copyright owners, who will determine whether, and under what conditions, including fees and charges, the materials in this book may be used them. In other words, a licensing facility exists for the legitimate use of the material in this book on other than an individual basis. However, it is asseverated and affirmed here that the material in this book CANNOT be used without the receipt of the express permission of such a licensing agreement from the Publishers. Inquiries re licensing should be addressed to the company, attention rights and permissions department.

All rights reserved, including the right of reproduction in whole or in part, in any form or by any means, electronic or mechanical, including photocopying, recording, or by any information storage and retrieval system, without permission in writing from the Publisher.

Copyright © 2024 by
National Learning Corporation

212 Michael Drive, Syosset, NY 11791
(516) 921-8888 • www.passbooks.com
E-mail: info@passbooks.com

PUBLISHED IN THE UNITED STATES OF AMERICA

PASSBOOK® SERIES

THE *PASSBOOK® SERIES* has been created to prepare applicants and candidates for the ultimate academic battlefield – the examination room.

At some time in our lives, each and every one of us may be required to take an examination – for validation, matriculation, admission, qualification, registration, certification, or licensure.

Based on the assumption that every applicant or candidate has met the basic formal educational standards, has taken the required number of courses, and read the necessary texts, the *PASSBOOK® SERIES* furnishes the one special preparation which may assure passing with confidence, instead of failing with insecurity. Examination questions – together with answers – are furnished as the basic vehicle for study so that the mysteries of the examination and its compounding difficulties may be eliminated or diminished by a sure method.

This book is meant to help you pass your examination provided that you qualify and are serious in your objective.

The entire field is reviewed through the huge store of content information which is succinctly presented through a provocative and challenging approach – the question-and-answer method.

A climate of success is established by furnishing the correct answers at the end of each test.

You soon learn to recognize types of questions, forms of questions, and patterns of questioning. You may even begin to anticipate expected outcomes.

You perceive that many questions are repeated or adapted so that you can gain acute insights, which may enable you to score many sure points.

You learn how to confront new questions, or types of questions, and to attack them confidently and work out the correct answers.

You note objectives and emphases, and recognize pitfalls and dangers, so that you may make positive educational adjustments.

Moreover, you are kept fully informed in relation to new concepts, methods, practices, and directions in the field.

You discover that you are actually taking the examination all the time: you are preparing for the examination by "taking" an examination, not by reading extraneous and/or supererogatory textbooks.

In short, this PASSBOOK®, used directedly, should be an important factor in helping you to pass your test.

HEATING PLANT TECHNICIAN

JOB DESCRIPTION
   Under supervision, operates heating and domestic hot water boilers in a public housing project; performs related work.

EXAMPLES OF TYPICAL TASKS
   Stands watch and fires low pressure boilers with heavy fuel oil. Maintains, adjusts, and makes minor repairs to boilers, industrial oil burners, heating and domestic hot water equipment and all auxiliaries. Keeps logs and makes reports as required.

TEST
   The multiple-choice test may include questions on the operation, maintenance and repair of boilers and related equipment and tools used in a low pressure boiler plant; proper work, environmental and safety boiler room practices; arithmetic; basic electrical and mechanical principals; piping; record keeping; standards of proper employee ethical conduct; and other related areas including written comprehension; written expression; number facility; and information ordering.

HOW TO TAKE A TEST

I. YOU MUST PASS AN EXAMINATION

A. *WHAT EVERY CANDIDATE SHOULD KNOW*

Examination applicants often ask us for help in preparing for the written test. What can I study in advance? What kinds of questions will be asked? How will the test be given? How will the papers be graded?

As an applicant for a civil service examination, you may be wondering about some of these things. Our purpose here is to suggest effective methods of advance study and to describe civil service examinations.

Your chances for success on this examination can be increased if you know how to prepare. Those "pre-examination jitters" can be reduced if you know what to expect. You can even experience an adventure in good citizenship if you know why civil service exams are given.

B. *WHY ARE CIVIL SERVICE EXAMINATIONS GIVEN?*

Civil service examinations are important to you in two ways. As a citizen, you want public jobs filled by employees who know how to do their work. As a job seeker, you want a fair chance to compete for that job on an equal footing with other candidates. The best-known means of accomplishing this two-fold goal is the competitive examination.

Exams are widely publicized throughout the nation. They may be administered for jobs in federal, state, city, municipal, town or village governments or agencies.

Any citizen may apply, with some limitations, such as the age or residence of applicants. Your experience and education may be reviewed to see whether you meet the requirements for the particular examination. When these requirements exist, they are reasonable and applied consistently to all applicants. Thus, a competitive examination may cause you some uneasiness now, but it is your privilege and safeguard.

C. *HOW ARE CIVIL SERVICE EXAMS DEVELOPED?*

Examinations are carefully written by trained technicians who are specialists in the field known as "psychological measurement," in consultation with recognized authorities in the field of work that the test will cover. These experts recommend the subject matter areas or skills to be tested; only those knowledges or skills important to your success on the job are included. The most reliable books and source materials available are used as references. Together, the experts and technicians judge the difficulty level of the questions.

Test technicians know how to phrase questions so that the problem is clearly stated. Their ethics do not permit "trick" or "catch" questions. Questions may have been tried out on sample groups, or subjected to statistical analysis, to determine their usefulness.

Written tests are often used in combination with performance tests, ratings of training and experience, and oral interviews. All of these measures combine to form the best-known means of finding the right person for the right job.

II. HOW TO PASS THE WRITTEN TEST

A. NATURE OF THE EXAMINATION

To prepare intelligently for civil service examinations, you should know how they differ from school examinations you have taken. In school you were assigned certain definite pages to read or subjects to cover. The examination questions were quite detailed and usually emphasized memory. Civil service exams, on the other hand, try to discover your present ability to perform the duties of a position, plus your potentiality to learn these duties. In other words, a civil service exam attempts to predict how successful you will be. Questions cover such a broad area that they cannot be as minute and detailed as school exam questions.

In the public service similar kinds of work, or positions, are grouped together in one "class." This process is known as *position-classification*. All the positions in a class are paid according to the salary range for that class. One class title covers all of these positions, and they are all tested by the same examination.

B. FOUR BASIC STEPS

1) Study the announcement

How, then, can you know what subjects to study? Our best answer is: "Learn as much as possible about the class of positions for which you've applied." The exam will test the knowledge, skills and abilities needed to do the work.

Your most valuable source of information about the position you want is the official exam announcement. This announcement lists the training and experience qualifications. Check these standards and apply only if you come reasonably close to meeting them.

The brief description of the position in the examination announcement offers some clues to the subjects which will be tested. Think about the job itself. Review the duties in your mind. Can you perform them, or are there some in which you are rusty? Fill in the blank spots in your preparation.

Many jurisdictions preview the written test in the exam announcement by including a section called "Knowledge and Abilities Required," "Scope of the Examination," or some similar heading. Here you will find out specifically what fields will be tested.

2) Review your own background

Once you learn in general what the position is all about, and what you need to know to do the work, ask yourself which subjects you already know fairly well and which need improvement. You may wonder whether to concentrate on improving your strong areas or on building some background in your fields of weakness. When the announcement has specified "some knowledge" or "considerable knowledge," or has used adjectives like "beginning principles of…" or "advanced … methods," you can get a clue as to the number and difficulty of questions to be asked in any given field. More questions, and hence broader coverage, would be included for those subjects which are more important in the work. Now weigh your strengths and weaknesses against the job requirements and prepare accordingly.

3) Determine the level of the position

Another way to tell how intensively you should prepare is to understand the level of the job for which you are applying. Is it the entering level? In other words, is this the position in which beginners in a field of work are hired? Or is it an intermediate or advanced level? Sometimes this is indicated by such words as "Junior" or "Senior" in the class title. Other jurisdictions use Roman numerals to designate the level – Clerk I, Clerk II, for example. The word "Supervisor" sometimes appears in the title. If the level is not indicated by the title, check the description of duties. Will you be working under very close supervision, or will you have responsibility for independent decisions in this work?

4) Choose appropriate study materials

Now that you know the subjects to be examined and the relative amount of each subject to be covered, you can choose suitable study materials. For beginning level jobs, or even advanced ones, if you have a pronounced weakness in some aspect of your training, read a modern, standard textbook in that field. Be sure it is up to date and has general coverage. Such books are normally available at your library, and the librarian will be glad to help you locate one. For entry-level positions, questions of appropriate difficulty are chosen – neither highly advanced questions, nor those too simple. Such questions require careful thought but not advanced training.

If the position for which you are applying is technical or advanced, you will read more advanced, specialized material. If you are already familiar with the basic principles of your field, elementary textbooks would waste your time. Concentrate on advanced textbooks and technical periodicals. Think through the concepts and review difficult problems in your field.

These are all general sources. You can get more ideas on your own initiative, following these leads. For example, training manuals and publications of the government agency which employs workers in your field can be useful, particularly for technical and professional positions. A letter or visit to the government department involved may result in more specific study suggestions, and certainly will provide you with a more definite idea of the exact nature of the position you are seeking.

III. KINDS OF TESTS

Tests are used for purposes other than measuring knowledge and ability to perform specified duties. For some positions, it is equally important to test ability to make adjustments to new situations or to profit from training. In others, basic mental abilities not dependent on information are essential. Questions which test these things may not appear as pertinent to the duties of the position as those which test for knowledge and information. Yet they are often highly important parts of a fair examination. For very general questions, it is almost impossible to help you direct your study efforts. What we can do is to point out some of the more common of these general abilities needed in public service positions and describe some typical questions.

1) General information

Broad, general information has been found useful for predicting job success in some kinds of work. This is tested in a variety of ways, from vocabulary lists to questions about current events. Basic background in some field of work, such as sociology or economics, may be sampled in a group of questions. Often these are principles which have become familiar to most persons through exposure rather than through formal training. It is difficult to advise you how to study for these questions; being alert to the world around you is our best suggestion.

2) Verbal ability

An example of an ability needed in many positions is verbal or language ability. Verbal ability is, in brief, the ability to use and understand words. Vocabulary and grammar tests are typical measures of this ability. Reading comprehension or paragraph interpretation questions are common in many kinds of civil service tests. You are given a paragraph of written material and asked to find its central meaning.

3) Numerical ability

Number skills can be tested by the familiar arithmetic problem, by checking paired lists of numbers to see which are alike and which are different, or by interpreting charts and graphs. In the latter test, a graph may be printed in the test booklet which you are asked to use as the basis for answering questions.

4) Observation

A popular test for law-enforcement positions is the observation test. A picture is shown to you for several minutes, then taken away. Questions about the picture test your ability to observe both details and larger elements.

5) Following directions

In many positions in the public service, the employee must be able to carry out written instructions dependably and accurately. You may be given a chart with several columns, each column listing a variety of information. The questions require you to carry out directions involving the information given in the chart.

6) Skills and aptitudes

Performance tests effectively measure some manual skills and aptitudes. When the skill is one in which you are trained, such as typing or shorthand, you can practice. These tests are often very much like those given in business school or high school courses. For many of the other skills and aptitudes, however, no short-time preparation can be made. Skills and abilities natural to you or that you have developed throughout your lifetime are being tested.

Many of the general questions just described provide all the data needed to answer the questions and ask you to use your reasoning ability to find the answers. Your best preparation for these tests, as well as for tests of facts and ideas, is to be at your physical and mental best. You, no doubt, have your own methods of getting into an exam-taking mood and keeping "in shape." The next section lists some ideas on this subject.

IV. KINDS OF QUESTIONS

Only rarely is the "essay" question, which you answer in narrative form, used in civil service tests. Civil service tests are usually of the short-answer type. Full instructions for answering these questions will be given to you at the examination. But in case this is your first experience with short-answer questions and separate answer sheets, here is what you need to know:

1) **Multiple-choice Questions**

Most popular of the short-answer questions is the "multiple choice" or "best answer" question. It can be used, for example, to test for factual knowledge, ability to solve problems or judgment in meeting situations found at work.

A multiple-choice question is normally one of three types—
- It can begin with an incomplete statement followed by several possible endings. You are to find the one ending which *best* completes the statement, although some of the others may not be entirely wrong.
- It can also be a complete statement in the form of a question which is answered by choosing one of the statements listed.

- It can be in the form of a problem – again you select the best answer.

Here is an example of a multiple-choice question with a discussion which should give you some clues as to the method for choosing the right answer:

When an employee has a complaint about his assignment, the action which will *best* help him overcome his difficulty is to
- A. discuss his difficulty with his coworkers
- B. take the problem to the head of the organization
- C. take the problem to the person who gave him the assignment
- D. say nothing to anyone about his complaint

In answering this question, you should study each of the choices to find which is best. Consider choice "A" – Certainly an employee may discuss his complaint with fellow employees, but no change or improvement can result, and the complaint remains unresolved. Choice "B" is a poor choice since the head of the organization probably does not know what assignment you have been given, and taking your problem to him is known as "going over the head" of the supervisor. The supervisor, or person who made the assignment, is the person who can clarify it or correct any injustice. Choice "C" is, therefore, correct. To say nothing, as in choice "D," is unwise. Supervisors have and interest in knowing the problems employees are facing, and the employee is seeking a solution to his problem.

2) True/False Questions

The "true/false" or "right/wrong" form of question is sometimes used. Here a complete statement is given. Your job is to decide whether the statement is right or wrong.

SAMPLE: A roaming cell-phone call to a nearby city costs less than a non-roaming call to a distant city.

This statement is wrong, or false, since roaming calls are more expensive.

This is not a complete list of all possible question forms, although most of the others are variations of these common types. You will always get complete directions for answering questions. Be sure you understand *how* to mark your answers – ask questions until you do.

V. RECORDING YOUR ANSWERS

Computer terminals are used more and more today for many different kinds of exams.

For an examination with very few applicants, you may be told to record your answers in the test booklet itself. Separate answer sheets are much more common. If this separate answer sheet is to be scored by machine – and this is often the case – it is highly important that you mark your answers correctly in order to get credit.

An electronic scoring machine is often used in civil service offices because of the speed with which papers can be scored. Machine-scored answer sheets must be marked with a pencil, which will be given to you. This pencil has a high graphite content which responds to the electronic scoring machine. As a matter of fact, stray dots may register as answers, so do not let your pencil rest on the answer sheet while you are pondering the correct answer. Also, if your pencil lead breaks or is otherwise defective, ask for another.

Since the answer sheet will be dropped in a slot in the scoring machine, be careful not to bend the corners or get the paper crumpled.

The answer sheet normally has five vertical columns of numbers, with 30 numbers to a column. These numbers correspond to the question numbers in your test booklet. After each number, going across the page are four or five pairs of dotted lines. These short dotted lines have small letters or numbers above them. The first two pairs may also have a "T" or "F" above the letters. This indicates that the first two pairs only are to be used if the questions are of the true-false type. If the questions are multiple choice, disregard the "T" and "F" and pay attention only to the small letters or numbers.

Answer your questions in the manner of the sample that follows:

32. The largest city in the United States is
    A. Washington, D.C.
    B. New York City
    C. Chicago
    D. Detroit
    E. San Francisco

1) Choose the answer you think is best. (New York City is the largest, so "B" is correct.)
2) Find the row of dotted lines numbered the same as the question you are answering. (Find row number 32)
3) Find the pair of dotted lines corresponding to the answer. (Find the pair of lines under the mark "B.")
4) Make a solid black mark between the dotted lines.

VI. BEFORE THE TEST

Common sense will help you find procedures to follow to get ready for an examination. Too many of us, however, overlook these sensible measures. Indeed, nervousness and fatigue have been found to be the most serious reasons why applicants fail to do their best on civil service tests. Here is a list of reminders:

- Begin your preparation early – Don't wait until the last minute to go scurrying around for books and materials or to find out what the position is all about.
- Prepare continuously – An hour a night for a week is better than an all-night cram session. This has been definitely established. What is more, a night a week for a month will return better dividends than crowding your study into a shorter period of time.
- Locate the place of the exam – You have been sent a notice telling you when and where to report for the examination. If the location is in a different town or otherwise unfamiliar to you, it would be well to inquire the best route and learn something about the building.
- Relax the night before the test – Allow your mind to rest. Do not study at all that night. Plan some mild recreation or diversion; then go to bed early and get a good night's sleep.
- Get up early enough to make a leisurely trip to the place for the test – This way unforeseen events, traffic snarls, unfamiliar buildings, etc. will not upset you.
- Dress comfortably – A written test is not a fashion show. You will be known by number and not by name, so wear something comfortable.

- Leave excess paraphernalia at home – Shopping bags and odd bundles will get in your way. You need bring only the items mentioned in the official notice you received; usually everything you need is provided. Do not bring reference books to the exam. They will only confuse those last minutes and be taken away from you when in the test room.
- Arrive somewhat ahead of time – If because of transportation schedules you must get there very early, bring a newspaper or magazine to take your mind off yourself while waiting.
- Locate the examination room – When you have found the proper room, you will be directed to the seat or part of the room where you will sit. Sometimes you are given a sheet of instructions to read while you are waiting. Do not fill out any forms until you are told to do so; just read them and be prepared.
- Relax and prepare to listen to the instructions
- If you have any physical problem that may keep you from doing your best, be sure to tell the test administrator. If you are sick or in poor health, you really cannot do your best on the exam. You can come back and take the test some other time.

VII. AT THE TEST

The day of the test is here and you have the test booklet in your hand. The temptation to get going is very strong. Caution! There is more to success than knowing the right answers. You must know how to identify your papers and understand variations in the type of short-answer question used in this particular examination. Follow these suggestions for maximum results from your efforts:

1) Cooperate with the monitor

The test administrator has a duty to create a situation in which you can be as much at ease as possible. He will give instructions, tell you when to begin, check to see that you are marking your answer sheet correctly, and so on. He is not there to guard you, although he will see that your competitors do not take unfair advantage. He wants to help you do your best.

2) Listen to all instructions

Don't jump the gun! Wait until you understand all directions. In most civil service tests you get more time than you need to answer the questions. So don't be in a hurry. Read each word of instructions until you clearly understand the meaning. Study the examples, listen to all announcements and follow directions. Ask questions if you do not understand what to do.

3) Identify your papers

Civil service exams are usually identified by number only. You will be assigned a number; you must not put your name on your test papers. Be sure to copy your number correctly. Since more than one exam may be given, copy your exact examination title.

4) Plan your time

Unless you are told that a test is a "speed" or "rate of work" test, speed itself is usually not important. Time enough to answer all the questions will be provided, but this does not mean that you have all day. An overall time limit has been set. Divide the total time (in minutes) by the number of questions to determine the approximate time you have for each question.

5) Do not linger over difficult questions

If you come across a difficult question, mark it with a paper clip (useful to have along) and come back to it when you have been through the booklet. One caution if you do this – be sure to skip a number on your answer sheet as well. Check often to be sure that you have not lost your place and that you are marking in the row numbered the same as the question you are answering.

6) Read the questions

Be sure you know what the question asks! Many capable people are unsuccessful because they failed to *read* the questions correctly.

7) Answer all questions

Unless you have been instructed that a penalty will be deducted for incorrect answers, it is better to guess than to omit a question.

8) Speed tests

It is often better NOT to guess on speed tests. It has been found that on timed tests people are tempted to spend the last few seconds before time is called in marking answers at random – without even reading them – in the hope of picking up a few extra points. To discourage this practice, the instructions may warn you that your score will be "corrected" for guessing. That is, a penalty will be applied. The incorrect answers will be deducted from the correct ones, or some other penalty formula will be used.

9) Review your answers

If you finish before time is called, go back to the questions you guessed or omitted to give them further thought. Review other answers if you have time.

10) Return your test materials

If you are ready to leave before others have finished or time is called, take ALL your materials to the monitor and leave quietly. Never take any test material with you. The monitor can discover whose papers are not complete, and taking a test booklet may be grounds for disqualification.

VIII. EXAMINATION TECHNIQUES

1) Read the general instructions carefully. These are usually printed on the first page of the exam booklet. As a rule, these instructions refer to the timing of the examination; the fact that you should not start work until the signal and must stop work at a signal, etc. If there are any *special* instructions, such as a choice of questions to be answered, make sure that you note this instruction carefully.

2) When you are ready to start work on the examination, that is as soon as the signal has been given, read the instructions to each question booklet, underline any key words or phrases, such as *least, best, outline, describe* and the like. In this way you will tend to answer as requested rather than discover on reviewing your paper that you *listed without describing*, that you selected the *worst* choice rather than the *best* choice, etc.

3) If the examination is of the objective or multiple-choice type – that is, each question will also give a series of possible answers: A, B, C or D, and you are called upon to select the best answer and write the letter next to that answer on your answer paper – it is advisable to start answering each question in turn. There may be anywhere from 50 to 100 such questions in the three or four hours allotted and you can see how much time would be taken if you read through all the questions before beginning to answer any. Furthermore, if you come across a question or group of questions which you know would be difficult to answer, it would undoubtedly affect your handling of all the other questions.

4) If the examination is of the essay type and contains but a few questions, it is a moot point as to whether you should read all the questions before starting to answer any one. Of course, if you are given a choice – say five out of seven and the like – then it is essential to read all the questions so you can eliminate the two that are most difficult. If, however, you are asked to answer all the questions, there may be danger in trying to answer the easiest one first because you may find that you will spend too much time on it. The best technique is to answer the first question, then proceed to the second, etc.

5) Time your answers. Before the exam begins, write down the time it started, then add the time allowed for the examination and write down the time it must be completed, then divide the time available somewhat as follows:
    - If 3-1/2 hours are allowed, that would be 210 minutes. If you have 80 objective-type questions, that would be an average of 2-1/2 minutes per question. Allow yourself no more than 2 minutes per question, or a total of 160 minutes, which will permit about 50 minutes to review.
    - If for the time allotment of 210 minutes there are 7 essay questions to answer, that would average about 30 minutes a question. Give yourself only 25 minutes per question so that you have about 35 minutes to review.

6) The most important instruction is to *read each question* and make sure you know what is wanted. The second most important instruction is to *time yourself properly* so that you answer every question. The third most important instruction is to *answer every question*. Guess if you have to but include something for each question. Remember that you will receive no credit for a blank and will probably receive some credit if you write something in answer to an essay question. If you guess a letter – say "B" for a multiple-choice question – you may have guessed right. If you leave a blank as an answer to a multiple-choice question, the examiners may respect your feelings but it will not add a point to your score. Some exams may penalize you for wrong answers, so in such cases *only*, you may not want to guess unless you have some basis for your answer.

7) Suggestions
    a. Objective-type questions
        1. Examine the question booklet for proper sequence of pages and questions
        2. Read all instructions carefully
        3. Skip any question which seems too difficult; return to it after all other questions have been answered
        4. Apportion your time properly; do not spend too much time on any single question or group of questions

5. Note and underline key words – *all, most, fewest, least, best, worst, same, opposite,* etc.
6. Pay particular attention to negatives
7. Note unusual option, e.g., unduly long, short, complex, different or similar in content to the body of the question
8. Observe the use of "hedging" words – *probably, may, most likely,* etc.
9. Make sure that your answer is put next to the same number as the question
10. Do not second-guess unless you have good reason to believe the second answer is definitely more correct
11. Cross out original answer if you decide another answer is more accurate; do not erase until you are ready to hand your paper in
12. Answer all questions; guess unless instructed otherwise
13. Leave time for review

b. Essay questions
1. Read each question carefully
2. Determine exactly what is wanted. Underline key words or phrases.
3. Decide on outline or paragraph answer
4. Include many different points and elements unless asked to develop any one or two points or elements
5. Show impartiality by giving pros and cons unless directed to select one side only
6. Make and write down any assumptions you find necessary to answer the questions
7. Watch your English, grammar, punctuation and choice of words
8. Time your answers; don't crowd material

8) Answering the essay question

Most essay questions can be answered by framing the specific response around several key words or ideas. Here are a few such key words or ideas:

M's: manpower, materials, methods, money, management
P's: purpose, program, policy, plan, procedure, practice, problems, pitfalls, personnel, public relations

a. Six basic steps in handling problems:
1. Preliminary plan and background development
2. Collect information, data and facts
3. Analyze and interpret information, data and facts
4. Analyze and develop solutions as well as make recommendations
5. Prepare report and sell recommendations
6. Install recommendations and follow up effectiveness

b. Pitfalls to avoid
1. *Taking things for granted* – A statement of the situation does not necessarily imply that each of the elements is necessarily true; for example, a complaint may be invalid and biased so that all that can be taken for granted is that a complaint has been registered

2. *Considering only one side of a situation* – Wherever possible, indicate several alternatives and then point out the reasons you selected the best one
3. *Failing to indicate follow up* – Whenever your answer indicates action on your part, make certain that you will take proper follow-up action to see how successful your recommendations, procedures or actions turn out to be
4. *Taking too long in answering any single question* – Remember to time your answers properly

IX. AFTER THE TEST

Scoring procedures differ in detail among civil service jurisdictions although the general principles are the same. Whether the papers are hand-scored or graded by machine we have described, they are nearly always graded by number. That is, the person who marks the paper knows only the number – never the name – of the applicant. Not until all the papers have been graded will they be matched with names. If other tests, such as training and experience or oral interview ratings have been given, scores will be combined. Different parts of the examination usually have different weights. For example, the written test might count 60 percent of the final grade, and a rating of training and experience 40 percent. In many jurisdictions, veterans will have a certain number of points added to their grades.

After the final grade has been determined, the names are placed in grade order and an eligible list is established. There are various methods for resolving ties between those who get the same final grade – probably the most common is to place first the name of the person whose application was received first. Job offers are made from the eligible list in the order the names appear on it. You will be notified of your grade and your rank as soon as all these computations have been made. This will be done as rapidly as possible.

People who are found to meet the requirements in the announcement are called "eligibles." Their names are put on a list of eligible candidates. An eligible's chances of getting a job depend on how high he stands on this list and how fast agencies are filling jobs from the list.

When a job is to be filled from a list of eligibles, the agency asks for the names of people on the list of eligibles for that job. When the civil service commission receives this request, it sends to the agency the names of the three people highest on this list. Or, if the job to be filled has specialized requirements, the office sends the agency the names of the top three persons who meet these requirements from the general list.

The appointing officer makes a choice from among the three people whose names were sent to him. If the selected person accepts the appointment, the names of the others are put back on the list to be considered for future openings.

That is the rule in hiring from all kinds of eligible lists, whether they are for typist, carpenter, chemist, or something else. For every vacancy, the appointing officer has his choice of any one of the top three eligibles on the list. This explains why the person whose name is on top of the list sometimes does not get an appointment when some of the persons lower on the list do. If the appointing officer chooses the second or third eligible, the No. 1 eligible does not get a job at once, but stays on the list until he is appointed or the list is terminated.

X. HOW TO PASS THE INTERVIEW TEST

The examination for which you applied requires an oral interview test. You have already taken the written test and you are now being called for the interview test – the final part of the formal examination.

You may think that it is not possible to prepare for an interview test and that there are no procedures to follow during an interview. Our purpose is to point out some things you can do in advance that will help you and some good rules to follow and pitfalls to avoid while you are being interviewed.

What is an interview supposed to test?

The written examination is designed to test the technical knowledge and competence of the candidate; the oral is designed to evaluate intangible qualities, not readily measured otherwise, and to establish a list showing the relative fitness of each candidate – as measured against his competitors – for the position sought. Scoring is not on the basis of "right" and "wrong," but on a sliding scale of values ranging from "not passable" to "outstanding." As a matter of fact, it is possible to achieve a relatively low score without a single "incorrect" answer because of evident weakness in the qualities being measured.

Occasionally, an examination may consist entirely of an oral test – either an individual or a group oral. In such cases, information is sought concerning the technical knowledges and abilities of the candidate, since there has been no written examination for this purpose. More commonly, however, an oral test is used to supplement a written examination.

Who conducts interviews?

The composition of oral boards varies among different jurisdictions. In nearly all, a representative of the personnel department serves as chairman. One of the members of the board may be a representative of the department in which the candidate would work. In some cases, "outside experts" are used, and, frequently, a businessman or some other representative of the general public is asked to serve. Labor and management or other special groups may be represented. The aim is to secure the services of experts in the appropriate field.

However the board is composed, it is a good idea (and not at all improper or unethical) to ascertain in advance of the interview who the members are and what groups they represent. When you are introduced to them, you will have some idea of their backgrounds and interests, and at least you will not stutter and stammer over their names.

What should be done before the interview?

While knowledge about the board members is useful and takes some of the surprise element out of the interview, there is other preparation which is more substantive. It *is* possible to prepare for an oral interview – in several ways:

1) Keep a copy of your application and review it carefully before the interview

This may be the only document before the oral board, and the starting point of the interview. Know what education and experience you have listed there, and the sequence and dates of all of it. Sometimes the board will ask you to review the highlights of your experience for them; you should not have to hem and haw doing it.

2) Study the class specification and the examination announcement

Usually, the oral board has one or both of these to guide them. The qualities, characteristics or knowledges required by the position sought are stated in these documents. They offer valuable clues as to the nature of the oral interview. For example, if the job involves supervisory responsibilities, the announcement will usually indicate that knowledge of modern supervisory methods and the qualifications of the candidate as a supervisor will be tested. If so, you can expect such questions, frequently in the form of a hypothetical situation which you are expected to solve. NEVER go into an oral without knowledge of the duties and responsibilities of the job you seek.

3) Think through each qualification required

Try to visualize the kind of questions you would ask if you were a board member. How well could you answer them? Try especially to appraise your own knowledge and background in each area, *measured against the job sought*, and identify any areas in which you are weak. Be critical and realistic – do not flatter yourself.

4) Do some general reading in areas in which you feel you may be weak

For example, if the job involves supervision and your past experience has NOT, some general reading in supervisory methods and practices, particularly in the field of human relations, might be useful. Do NOT study agency procedures or detailed manuals. The oral board will be testing your understanding and capacity, not your memory.

5) Get a good night's sleep and watch your general health and mental attitude

You will want a clear head at the interview. Take care of a cold or any other minor ailment, and of course, no hangovers.

What should be done on the day of the interview?

Now comes the day of the interview itself. Give yourself plenty of time to get there. Plan to arrive somewhat ahead of the scheduled time, particularly if your appointment is in the fore part of the day. If a previous candidate fails to appear, the board might be ready for you a bit early. By early afternoon an oral board is almost invariably behind schedule if there are many candidates, and you may have to wait. Take along a book or magazine to read, or your application to review, but leave any extraneous material in the waiting room when you go in for your interview. In any event, relax and compose yourself.

The matter of dress is important. The board is forming impressions about you – from your experience, your manners, your attitude, and your appearance. Give your personal appearance careful attention. Dress your best, but not your flashiest. Choose conservative, appropriate clothing, and be sure it is immaculate. This is a business interview, and your appearance should indicate that you regard it as such. Besides, being well groomed and properly dressed will help boost your confidence.

Sooner or later, someone will call your name and escort you into the interview room. *This is it.* From here on you are on your own. It is too late for any more preparation. But remember, you asked for this opportunity to prove your fitness, and you are here because your request was granted.

What happens when you go in?

The usual sequence of events will be as follows: The clerk (who is often the board stenographer) will introduce you to the chairman of the oral board, who will introduce you to the other members of the board. Acknowledge the introductions before you sit down. Do not be surprised if you find a microphone facing you or a stenotypist sitting by. Oral interviews are usually recorded in the event of an appeal or other review.

Usually the chairman of the board will open the interview by reviewing the highlights of your education and work experience from your application – primarily for the benefit of the other members of the board, as well as to get the material into the record. Do not interrupt or comment unless there is an error or significant misinterpretation; if that is the case, do not hesitate. But do not quibble about insignificant matters. Also, he will usually ask you some question about your education, experience or your present job – partly to get you to start talking and to establish the interviewing "rapport." He may start the actual questioning, or turn it over to one of the other members. Frequently, each member undertakes the questioning on a particular area, one in which he is perhaps most competent, so you can expect each member to participate in the examination. Because time is limited, you may also expect some rather abrupt switches in the direction the questioning takes, so do not be upset by it. Normally, a board member will not pursue a single line of questioning unless he discovers a particular strength or weakness.

After each member has participated, the chairman will usually ask whether any member has any further questions, then will ask you if you have anything you wish to add. Unless you are expecting this question, it may floor you. Worse, it may start you off on an extended, extemporaneous speech. The board is not usually seeking more information. The question is principally to offer you a last opportunity to present further qualifications or to indicate that you have nothing to add. So, if you feel that a significant qualification or characteristic has been overlooked, it is proper to point it out in a sentence or so. Do not compliment the board on the thoroughness of their examination – they have been sketchy, and you know it. If you wish, merely say, "No thank you, I have nothing further to add." This is a point where you can "talk yourself out" of a good impression or fail to present an important bit of information. Remember, *you close the interview yourself*.

The chairman will then say, "That is all, Mr. _____, thank you." Do not be startled; the interview is over, and quicker than you think. Thank him, gather your belongings and take your leave. Save your sigh of relief for the other side of the door.

How to put your best foot forward

Throughout this entire process, you may feel that the board individually and collectively is trying to pierce your defenses, seek out your hidden weaknesses and embarrass and confuse you. Actually, this is not true. They are obliged to make an appraisal of your qualifications for the job you are seeking, and they want to see you in your best light. Remember, they must interview all candidates and a non-cooperative candidate may become a failure in spite of their best efforts to bring out his qualifications. Here are 15 suggestions that will help you:

1) Be natural – Keep your attitude confident, not cocky

If you are not confident that you can do the job, do not expect the board to be. Do not apologize for your weaknesses, try to bring out your strong points. The board is interested in a positive, not negative, presentation. Cockiness will antagonize any board member and make him wonder if you are covering up a weakness by a false show of strength.

2) Get comfortable, but don't lounge or sprawl

Sit erectly but not stiffly. A careless posture may lead the board to conclude that you are careless in other things, or at least that you are not impressed by the importance of the occasion. Either conclusion is natural, even if incorrect. Do not fuss with your clothing, a pencil or an ashtray. Your hands may occasionally be useful to emphasize a point; do not let them become a point of distraction.

3) Do not wisecrack or make small talk

This is a serious situation, and your attitude should show that you consider it as such. Further, the time of the board is limited – they do not want to waste it, and neither should you.

4) Do not exaggerate your experience or abilities

In the first place, from information in the application or other interviews and sources, the board may know more about you than you think. Secondly, you probably will not get away with it. An experienced board is rather adept at spotting such a situation, so do not take the chance.

5) If you know a board member, do not make a point of it, yet do not hide it

Certainly you are not fooling him, and probably not the other members of the board. Do not try to take advantage of your acquaintanceship – it will probably do you little good.

6) Do not dominate the interview

Let the board do that. They will give you the clues – do not assume that you have to do all the talking. Realize that the board has a number of questions to ask you, and do not try to take up all the interview time by showing off your extensive knowledge of the answer to the first one.

7) Be attentive

You only have 20 minutes or so, and you should keep your attention at its sharpest throughout. When a member is addressing a problem or question to you, give him your undivided attention. Address your reply principally to him, but do not exclude the other board members.

8) Do not interrupt

A board member may be stating a problem for you to analyze. He will ask you a question when the time comes. Let him state the problem, and wait for the question.

9) Make sure you understand the question

Do not try to answer until you are sure what the question is. If it is not clear, restate it in your own words or ask the board member to clarify it for you. However, do not haggle about minor elements.

10) Reply promptly but not hastily

A common entry on oral board rating sheets is "candidate responded readily," or "candidate hesitated in replies." Respond as promptly and quickly as you can, but do not jump to a hasty, ill-considered answer.

11) Do not be peremptory in your answers

A brief answer is proper – but do not fire your answer back. That is a losing game from your point of view. The board member can probably ask questions much faster than you can answer them.

12) Do not try to create the answer you think the board member wants

He is interested in what kind of mind you have and how it works – not in playing games. Furthermore, he can usually spot this practice and will actually grade you down on it.

13) Do not switch sides in your reply merely to agree with a board member

Frequently, a member will take a contrary position merely to draw you out and to see if you are willing and able to defend your point of view. Do not start a debate, yet do not surrender a good position. If a position is worth taking, it is worth defending.

14) Do not be afraid to admit an error in judgment if you are shown to be wrong

The board knows that you are forced to reply without any opportunity for careful consideration. Your answer may be demonstrably wrong. If so, admit it and get on with the interview.

15) Do not dwell at length on your present job

The opening question may relate to your present assignment. Answer the question but do not go into an extended discussion. You are being examined for a *new* job, not your present one. As a matter of fact, try to phrase ALL your answers in terms of the job for which you are being examined.

Basis of Rating

Probably you will forget most of these "do's" and "don'ts" when you walk into the oral interview room. Even remembering them all will not ensure you a passing grade. Perhaps you did not have the qualifications in the first place. But remembering them will help you to put your best foot forward, without treading on the toes of the board members.

Rumor and popular opinion to the contrary notwithstanding, an oral board wants you to make the best appearance possible. They know you are under pressure – but they also want to see how you respond to it as a guide to what your reaction would be under the pressures of the job you seek. They will be influenced by the degree of poise you display, the personal traits you show and the manner in which you respond.

ABOUT THIS BOOK

This book contains tests divided into Examination Sections. Go through each test, answering every question in the margin. We have also attached a sample answer sheet at the back of the book that can be removed and used. At the end of each test look at the answer key and check your answers. On the ones you got wrong, look at the right answer choice and learn. Do not fill in the answers first. Do not memorize the questions and answers, but understand the answer and principles involved. On your test, the questions will likely be different from the samples. Questions are changed and new ones added. If you understand these past questions you should have success with any changes that arise. Tests may consist of several types of questions. We have additional books on each subject should more study be advisable or necessary for you. Finally, the more you study, the better prepared you will be. This book is intended to be the last thing you study before you walk into the examination room. Prior study of relevant texts is also recommended. NLC publishes some of these in our Fundamental Series. Knowledge and good sense are important factors in passing your exam. Good luck also helps. So now study this Passbook, absorb the material contained within and take that knowledge into the examination. Then do your best to pass that exam.

EXAMINATION SECTION

EXAMINATION SECTION
TEST 1

DIRECTIONS: Each question or incomplete statement is followed by several suggested answers or completions. Select the one that BEST answers the question or completes the statement. *PRINT THE LETTER OF THE CORRECT ANSWER IN THE SPACE AT THE RIGHT.*

1. A boiler horsepower is NOT defined as

    A. the evaporation of 34.5 lbs. of water per hour
    B. 33,475 Btu's
    C. 12 square feet of heating surface
    D. 12,000 Btu's per hour

2. The MOST important valve on a boiler is the _____ valve.

    A. stop-check   B. blow-down
    C. safety   D. vacuum breaker

3. A fusible plug is a plug that is

    A. installed on boilers to protect the boiler from dangerously low water
    B. inserted into a leaky tube
    C. installed on a pipe after the pipe has been disconnected from the boiler
    D. none of the above

4. A fusible plug is constructed of

    A. solid brass   B. bronze *only*
    C. bronze and tin   D. stainless steel

5. The melting point of a fusible plug is _____ degrees F.

    A. 450   B. 375   C. 200   D. 100

6. The pressure limitation for a fusible plug is _____ psi.

    A. 175   B. 225   C. 250   D. 300

7. The fusible plugs in a boiler are NOT placed in

    A. the crown sheet of a locomotive boiler
    B. one of the tubes of a vertical boiler
    C. the tube sheet of an H.R.T. boiler
    D. the drum of a water tube boiler

8. The valve NOT necessary on a boiler is the

    A. safety   B. stop-check
    C. blow-down   D. angle

9. If a boiler generates 4,000 lbs. of steam per hour, _____ Safety valves are required

    A. 1   B. 2   C. 3   D. 4

10. A low-water cut-off

    A. cuts off all water to the boiler
    B. cuts off the water on a blow-off
    C. shuts off the fuel supply to the boiler in the event of low water in the boiler
    D. keeps the water level up

11. The purpose of a stop-check valve is to

    A. stop the flow of steam when there is no demand
    B. prevent the backflow of steam into the boiler in the event of boiler failure
    C. stop the condensate from entering the boiler
    D. inject steam into the lines

12. The purpose of a blow-off valve is to blow off

    A. excess steam
    B. soot from the boiler
    C. impurities from the lowest point of the boiler
    D. excess condensate entering the boiler

13. A *pig-tail* is installed on a steam line to

    A. prevent air from getting into the steam lines
    B. create a vacuum in the line
    C. put the gauge up higher so it may be visible to the engineer
    D. prevent live steam from damaging the steam gauge

14. A steam injector is used on a steam boiler to

    A. heat the oil before it enters the boiler
    B. inject steam into the line for velocity
    C. force water into the boiler
    D. inject air into the boiler

15. Two hydrometer gas valves are installed on a gas main

    A. to insure efficiency
    B. to increase the gas pressure
    C. so that if one valve fails to open, the other valve will open
    D. so that if one valve fails to open, the other valve will not open

16. The bottom blow-off on a water tube boiler is located

    A. just below the section drum
    B. in between the two upper drums
    C. under the boiler
    D. at the rear of the boiler on the mud drum

17. The dry pipe on a boiler is located

    A. just below the last row of tubes
    B. below the superheater
    C. at the top of the steam and water drum
    D. between the superheater and the engine

18. The purpose of a superheater is to 18.____

    A. remove excess moisture from the steam
    B. create dry steam
    C. permit the engine to run more efficiently with superheated steam
    D. all of the above

19. Water wall tubes are used 19.____

    A. to insure proper amounts of water to the boiler
    B. because the boiler must have a certain number of tubes per boiler horsepower
    C. to carry off the excess heat from the furnace walls
    D. to create more steam

20. At what degree are the readings on the Celsius and Fahrenheit scale the same? 20.____

    A. 100   B. 212
    C. 10 below zero   D. 40 below zero

21. At what temperature does water boil on the celsius scale? _____ degrees. 21.____

    A. 100   B. 175   C. 212   D. 273

22. *Sensible heat* is the 22.____

    A. quality of heat required to change the state or condition without a change in temperature
    B. heat which produces an increase in temperature, as distinguished from latent heat, which produces a change in state
    C. heat indicating how hot or cold a substance is
    D. none of these

23. All of the following are functions of a separator EXCEPT: To 23.____

    A. increase the quality of steam
    B. extract condensate from the steam
    C. extract any oil or impurities from the steam
    D. equalize the steam pressure

24. The instrument used to record air-flow to steam-flow relationship is a 24.____

    A. hydrometer   B. steam flow meter
    C. pryometer   D. velocity meter

25. The gasket suitable for a flange on an oil line operating at 300 degrees F. is a(n) _____ gasket. 25.____

    A. rubber   B. asbestos
    C. oil paper   D. metallic

26. You would NOT install a valve marked 300 W.O.G. on a(n) _____ line carrying 250 psi. 26.____

    A. steam   B. water   C. gas   D. oil

27. A cause of high stack temperature is

    A. poor combustion
    B. sooty or scaled tubes
    C. poor water circulation
    D. none of these

28. The purpose of a barometric damper is to

    A. *increase* the draft pressure in the boiler
    B. *increase* the CO_2, and *decrease* the CO
    C. *decrease* the CO_2, and *increase* the CO
    D. *decrease* the CO_2 at the boiler outlet

29. API degree refers to the

    A. stamping on the boiler plate
    B. viscosity of oil
    C. temperature of oil
    D. American Petroleum Institute

30. If a boiler has 1,000 square feet of heating surface, what would the boiler horsepower be, assuming 12 square feet per BHP?

    A. 83.3   B. 1,012   C. 1,200   D. 12,000

KEY (CORRECT ANSWERS)

1.	D	16.	D
2.	C	17.	C
3.	A	18.	D
4.	C	19.	C
5.	A	20.	D
6.	C	21.	A
7.	D	22.	B
8.	D	23.	D
9.	B	24.	B
10.	C	25.	B
11.	B	26.	A
12.	C	27.	D
13.	D	28.	D
14.	C	29.	B
15.	D	30.	A

TEST 2

DIRECTIONS: Each question or incomplete statement is followed by several suggested answers or completions. Select the one that BEST answers the question or completes the statement. *PRINT THE LETTER OF THE CORRECT ANSWER IN THE SPACE AT THE RIGHT.*

1. In setting the nozzle pressure on a boiler WITHOUT a manometer, in order to obtain the inches of water column you should take the ounces of gas pressure and multiply by   1.____

   A. 0.5781   B. 1.73   C. 3.1416   D. 33,475

2. How many safety valves are required on a boiler having at LEAST 500 square feet?   2.____

   A. 1   B. 2   C. 3   D. 4

3. The FIRST thing to do before attempting to make a *major* repair to a boiler is to   3.____

   A. check to see if there is a qualified person who can do the repairs
   B. make sure parts are available for the repairs
   C. notify the insurance carrier to send an inspector who will recommend how the repairs should be done
   D. notify the insurance company to recommend a company to do the repairs

4. Which of the following methods is NOT employed with domestic hot water systems?   4.____

   A. Upfeed risers with returns having no connections paralleling the risers
   B. One main upfeed riser without connections, supplying all down feed risers for all fixtures
   C. Upfeed risers without connections, supplying a down feed riser for all fixtures
   D. Upfeed risers with returns in other locations, with connections taken off both supply and return

5. A steam gauge should be connected to a high pressure steam line with a(n)   5.____

   A. coupling   B. syphon
   C. union   D. ell and coupling

6. Coal is composed of   6.____

   A. moisture   B. fixed ash or carbon
   C. volatile matters   D. all of the above

7. If absolute pressure is 215 psia, what is the equivalent gauge pressure in psig?   7.____

   A. 190   B. 195   C. 200   D. 205

8. The valve between the fuel oil heater and the burner valve is called the _____ valve.   8.____

   A. check   B. safety   C. root   D. stop

9. The purpose of a tube retarder is to   9.____

   A. help circulate the water around the tubes
   B. prevent sagging of the tubes
   C. slow down the water circulation around the tubes
   D. restrict the combustible gases from traveling at a great speed through the tubes, giving more heat on the water side of the boiler

10. On a Scotch Marine boiler, the sheets on the side of the combustion chamber are called _____ sheets.

    A. crown
    B. wrapper
    C. bridge wall
    D. dry

11. The *primary* purpose of a steam injector is to pump water into the

    A. boiler while being tested
    B. boiler after the main feed pump fails to operate
    C. main condenser
    D. none of these

12. The *proper* way to blow down the bottom blow-off is by

    A. letting the water level drop slightly
    B. increasing the steam pressure
    C. adding about 2" of water to the boiler above the normal level
    D. increasing the oil pressure

13. If oil or scale is present on boiler tubes, the result will be

    A. oxidation
    B. overheating
    C. galvanic action
    D. over-lubrication

14. To maintain the proper water level on a manually-controlled feedwater system, you should

    A. operate the feed-check valve
    B. open the recirculating valve
    C. start the secondary feed pump
    D. open the feed pump stem valve

15. If the water in the sight glass is empty, you should

    A. add another feed pump on the line
    B. replace the check valve
    C. secure all burners
    D. close the feed stop valve

16. On a water tube boiler, the internal feed line is located at the

    A. top of the bottom drum
    B. top of the furnace
    C. bottom of the steam and water drum
    D. top of the steam and water drum

17. It is legal to install a Y branch fitting on a boiler

    A. on the water and steam drum
    B. in the combustion chamber
    C. on the wrapper sheet
    D. on the feedwater circulating pump

18. The purpose of a surface blow-down valve is to

    A. remove sludge and scale from the boiler
    B. blow down excess water if the level is too high
    C. remove all oil and scum from the surface
    D. help drain the boiler

19. A main condenser is used to

    A. convert steam into water
    B. convert water into steam
    C. increase the back pressure for better efficiency
    D. remove all air from the air chamber

20. If the condenser vacuum feed valve were left open, it would result in

    A. loss of condensate water
    B. vacuum loss
    C. intermittent loss of vacuum
    D. all of the above

21. A safety valve should be installed

    A. with a union
    B. with a coupling
    C. on top of a gate valve
    D. on the boiler without any other valve between the safety valve and the boiler

22. A stop or non-return valve

    A. is a valve attached to the steam outlet of a boiler which will close automatically if there is a pressure part failure in the boiler
    B. is used to prevent backflow of steam from the steam header to the point of failure
    C. will isolate automatically a defective boiler supplying steam to the same header
    D. all of the above

23. A blow-off valve is used to

    A. discharge mud from the boiler
    B. discharge all scale and impurities from the boiler
    C. lower high water level
    D. all of the above

24. A *pop* or blow back ring is

    A. located on a blow-down valve
    B. located on a non-return valve
    C. located on an orsat device
    D. used to regulate the blow down or closing pressure of a safety valve

25. The blow back ring affects the opening pressure of a safety valve by

    A. increasing the back pressure
    B. relieving the counter balance of any pressure
    C. affecting the closing pressure only, NOT the opening pressure
    D. helping to relieve the pressure quickly

26. The MOST common breakdowns in a boiler are in

    A. bulges in the shell
    B. leaky or split tubes
    C. faulty staybolts
    D. all of the above

27. Cracks *normally* occur

    A. around the rivet holes
    B. at flanged corners
    C. between tube openings
    D. all of the above

28. Repairs of cracks should be made by

    A. cutting the crack a little bigger, then welding it
    B. drilling small holes in each corner of the crack, preventing further extension, then patching over the crack
    C. cutting out a section in the shape of a square, then welding a patch either inside or outside
    D. none of the above

29. A hydrokineter is a(n)

    A. nozzle located inside a scotch marine boiler which helps circulate cool water while steam is blowing through the nozzle
    B. nozzle on the bottom of a scotch marine boiler to extract boiler water for testing
    C. instrument used with a salinity indicator
    D. instrument for measuring high temperatures

30. A manometer is an instrument used to measure

    A. draft and pressure by inches of water column
    B. air pressure
    C. amount of fuel
    D. the heating surface of a boiler

KEY (CORRECT ANSWERS)

1.	B	16.	C
2.	B	17.	A
3.	C	18.	C
4.	C	19.	A
5.	B	20.	C
6.	D	21.	D
7.	C	22.	D
8.	C	23.	D
9.	D	24.	D
10.	B	25.	C
11.	B	26.	D
12.	C	27.	D
13.	B	28.	B
14.	A	29.	A
15.	C	30.	A

TEST 3

DIRECTIONS: Each question or incomplete statement is followed by several suggested answers or completions. Select the one that BEST answers the question or completes the statement. *PRINT THE LETTER OF THE CORRECT ANSWER IN THE SPACE AT THE RIGHT.*

1. The MINIMUM size of pipe used on a blow-down connection on a high pressure boiler is 1.___

   A. 1½" B. 1 3/4" C. 2" D. 2½"

2. To convert cubic feet into pounds, multiply by 2.___

   A. 2.31 B. 1,728 C. 62.4 D. 144

3. Pressure is measured in 3.___

   A. cubic feet
   B. pounds per square inch
   C. pounds per square feet
   D. foot pounds

4. Pressure at sea level is _____ psi. 4.___

   A. 14.7 B. 15 C. 19 D. 25

5. Atmospheric pressure affects the operation of a steam engine by 5.___

   A. increasing the compression
   B. reducing the power and acting as a back pressure on the engine piston
   C. keeping the governor from lifting
   D. cutting back the exhaust

6. Atmospheric pressure can be relieved by 6.___

   A. using a back pressure valve
   B. using a condenser
   C. cutting back the pressure
   D. exhausting some of the pressure to the atmosphere

7. Atmospheric pressure is measured with a 7.___

   A. manometer B. pyrometer
   C. barometer D. hydrometer

8. The pressure of a low-pressure system is _____ psi. 8.___

   A. 10 B. 15 C. 25 D. 50

9. _____ draft is CORRECT for a boiler. 9.___

   A. Natural B. Forced
   C. Induced D. All of the above

10. Which of the following stays are IMPORTANT in the construction of a boiler? 10.___

    A. Gusset B. Rivet
    C. Diagonal D. All of the above

11. A ligament is the

   A. weld between two plates
   B. metal between a butt joint
   C. segment of tube sheet between the tubes
   D. metal between the back pitch

11.____

12. Water is cooled in a cooling tower by

   A. radiation
   B. convection
   C. evaporation
   D. all of the above

12.____

13. At LEAST _____ sq. ft. is needed to cool water in a cooling tower.

   A. 100   B. 175   C. 250   D. 1,000

13.____

14. A cooling tower is used to cool

   A. boiler condensate and extract impurities
   B. water for air conditioning
   C. water that is being returned to a boiler
   D. none of the above

14.____

15. To set the pressure on a safety valve use

   A. the hydrostatic method
   B. the gauge pressure on the boiler
   C. pneumatic pressure
   D. none of the above

15.____

16. If the pressure setting on a safety valve attached to a superheater is set to relieve at 200 psig, what should the pressure setting of the boiler safety valve be, in psig?

   A. 195   B. 200   C. 205   D. 225

16.____

17. There is sufficient amount of water in a boiler when

   A. the water in the gauge glass is filled to the top
   B. water starts to run out of the safety valve
   C. all the surface exposed to intense heat is submerged
   D. the boiler is half filled with water

17.____

18. To determine whether the boiler has the CORRECT level of water

   A. open the blow down valve, then check the water glass
   B. fill the boiler until the water glass is filled
   C. close the drain cock on the water glass until all the water has disappeared
   D. blow down the low water cut-off, then check the water glass for the true level

18.____

19. How much water should be carried in a vertical boiler?

   A. Half the boiler should be filled with water
   B. The water level should be 3" above the top row of tubes
   C. The water should be as high as possible without causing wet stream
   D. The water level should be about two thirds filled

19.____

20. The advantage of high water level in a vertical boiler is that it 20.____

    A. increases the efficiency of the tubular heating surface
    B. increases the steam space of the boiler
    C. produces superheated steam
    D. none of the above

21. A compound gauge measures 21.____

    A. ounces and water pressure
    B. vacuum and atmospheric pressure
    C. pressure and vacuum
    D. vacuum and absolute pressure

22. A steam gauge functions by 22.____

    A. steam pressure raising the gauge to the desired reading
    B. the expansion of a corrugated diaphragm when pressure is applied
    C. water and steam pressure combining to raise the pressure on the gauge
    D. none of the above

23. A water column 23.____

    A. indicates the pressure at the base
    B. contains a float which actuates a whistle when the water level drops below a safe level
    C. is installed on a condensate pump to indicate the amount of water in the receiver tank
    D. is a water gauge on a feedwater tank

24. How many gallons are there in an oil tank 10 feet high and 3 feet in diameter? 24.____

    A. 528.7   B. 5,089   C. 55,000   D. 508,940

25. What is the pressure in lbs., on the bottom of a feed-water tank filled with water, if it is 14 ft. long and 28 in. in diamerer? 25.____

    A. 3,600   B. 3,731   C. 4,275   D. 5,125

26. How many gallons are there in a tank 10 feet in diameter and 23 feet long? 26.____

    A. 11,700   B. 13,600   C. 15,800   D. none of these

27. What is the pressure in lbs., on the bottom of the tank in the preceding question? 27.____

    A. 95,000   B. 110,600   C. 112,563   D. 135,862

28. A city of 30,000 people consumes 1,500 gallons of water per minute from a holding tank of 250,000 gallons that is 200 feet high. 28.____
    What horsepower motor is required to replace this water, using the formula:

    $$HP = \frac{FOOT - POUNDS}{33,000 \, xt} \, ?$$

    A. 75 HP   B. 113 HP   C. 126 HP   D. 151 HP

29. To convert gallons of water to cubic feet, multiply by

   A. .1337   B. 3.785   C. 128   D. 231

30. The MAXIMUM theoretical lift of water at sea level is _____ feet.

   A. 12   B. 28   C. 34   D. 50

KEY (CORRECT ANSWERS)

1.	A	16.	C
2.	C	17.	C
3.	B	18.	D
4.	A	19.	C
5.	B	20.	A
6.	B	21.	C
7.	C	22.	B
8.	B	23.	B
9.	D	24.	A
10.	D	25.	B
11.	C	26.	D
12.	D	27.	C
13.	C	28.	C
14.	B	29.	A
15.	D	30.	C

EXAMINATION SECTION
TEST 1

DIRECTIONS: Each question or incomplete statement is followed by several suggested answers or completions. Select the one that BEST answers the question or completes the statement. *PRINT THE LETTER OF THE CORRECT ANSWER IN THE SPACE AT THE RIGHT.*

1. The combustion efficiency of a boiler can be determined with a CO_2 indicator and the

    A. under fire draft
    B. boiler room humidity
    C. flue gas temperature
    D. outside air temperature

    1.____

2. A quick, practical method of determining if the cast-iron waste pipe delivered to a job has been damaged in transit is to

    A. hydraulically test it
    B. "ring" each length with a hammer
    C. drop each length to see whether it breaks
    D. visually examine the pipe for cracks

    2.____

3. An electrostatic precipitator is used to

    A. filter the air supply
    B. remove sludge from the fuel oil
    C. remove particles from the fuel gas
    D. supply samples for an Orsat analysis

    3.____

4. The PRIMARY cause of cracking and spalling of refractory lining in the furnace of a steam generator is *most likely* due to

    A. continuous over-firing of boiler
    B. slag accumulation on furnace walls
    C. change in fuel from solid to liquid
    D. uneven heating and cooling within the refractory brick

    4.____

5. The term "effective temperature" in air conditioning means

    A. the dry bulb temperature
    B. the average of the wet and dry bulb temperatures
    C. the square root of the product of wet and dry bulb temperatures
    D. an arbitrary index combining the effects of temperature, humidity, and movement

    5.____

6. The piping in all buildings having dual water distribution systems should be identified by a color coding of _____ for potable water lines and _____ for non-potable water lines.

    A. green; red
    B. green; yellow
    C. yellow; green
    D. yellow; red

    6.____

7. The breaking of a component of a machine subjected to excessive vibration is called

    A. tensile failure
    B. fatigue failure
    C. caustic embrittlement
    D. amplitude failure

    7.____

8. The TWO MOST important factors to be considered in selecting fans for ventilating systems are

   A. noise and efficiency
   B. space available and weight
   C. first cost and dimensional bulk
   D. construction and arrangement of drive

9. In the modern power plant deaerator, air is removed from water to

   A. reduce heat losses in the heaters
   B. reduce corrosion of boiler steel due to the air
   C. reduce the load of the main condenser air pumps
   D. prevent pumps from becoming vapor bound

10. The abbreviations BOD, COD, and DO are associated with

    A. flue gas analysis
    B. air pollution control
    C. boiler water treatment
    D. water pollution control

11. The piping of a newly installed drainage system should be tested upon completion of the rough plumbing with a head of water of NOT LESS THAN _____ feet.

    A. 10   B. 15   C. 20   D. 25

12. Of the following statements concerning aquastats, the one which is CORRECT is:

    A. Aquastats may be obtained with either a narrow or wide range of settings
    B. Aquastats have a mercury tube switch which is controlled by the stack switch
    C. An aquastat is a device used to shut down the burner in the event of low water in the boiler
    D. An aquastat should be located about 4 inches above the normal water line of the boiler

13. The SAFEST way to protect the domestic water supply from contamination by sewage or non-potable water is to insert

    A. air gaps
    B. swing connections
    C. double check valves
    D. tanks with overhead discharge

14. The MAIN function of a back-pressure valve which is sometimes found in the connection between a water drain pipe and the sewer system is to

    A. equalize the pressure between the drain pipe and the sewer
    B. prevent sewer water from flowing into the drain pipe
    C. provide pressure to enable waste to reach the sewer
    D. make sure that there is not too much water pressure in the sewer line

15. Boiler water is neutral if its pH value is

    A. 0   B. 1   C. 7   D. 14

16. A domestic hot water mixing or tempering valve should be preceded in the hot water line by a

    A. strainer
    B. foot valve
    C. check valve
    D. steam trap

17. Between a steam boiler and its safety valve there should be

    A. no valve of any type
    B. a gate valve of the same size as the safety valve
    C. a swing check valve of at least the same size as the safety valve
    D. a cock having a clear opening equal in area to the pipe connecting the boiler and safety valve

18. A diagram of horizontal plumbing drainage lines should have cleanouts shown

    A. at least every 25 feet
    B. at least every 100 feet
    C. wherever a basin is located
    D. wherever a change in direction occurs

19. When a Bourdon gauge is used to measure steam pressures, some form of siphon or water seal must be maintained.
    The reason for this is to

    A. obtain "absolute" pressure readings
    B. prevent steam from entering the gage
    C. prevent condensate from entering the gage
    D. obtain readings below atmospheric pressure

20. In a closed heat exchanger, oil is cooled by condensate which is to be returned to a boiler. In order to avoid the possibility of contaminating the condensate with oil should a tube fail in the oil cooler, it would be good practice to

    A. cool the oil by air instead of water
    B. treat the condensate with an oil solvent
    C. keep the oil pressure in the exchanger higher than the water pressure
    D. keep the water pressure in the exchanger higher than the oil pressure

21. A radiator thermostatic trap is used on a vacuum return type of heating system to

    A. release the pocketed air only
    B. reduce the amount of condensate
    C. maintain a predetermined radiator water level
    D. prevent the return of live steam to the return line

22. According to the color coding of piping, fire protection piping should be painted

    A. green   B. yellow   C. purple   D. red

23. The MAIN purpose of a standpipe system is to

    A. supply the roof water tank
    B. provide water for firefighting

C. circulate water for the heating system
D. provide adequate pressure for the water supply

24. The name "Saybolt" is associated with the measurement of

    A. viscosity
    B. Btu content
    C. octane rating
    D. temperature

25. Recirculation of conditioned air in an air-conditioned building is done MAINLY to

    A. reduce refrigeration tonnage required
    B. increase room entrophy
    C. increase air specific humidity
    D. reduce room temperature below the dewpoint

26. In a plumbing installation, vent pipes are GENERALLY used to

    A. prevent the loss of water seal from traps by evaporation
    B. prevent the loss of water seal due to several causes other than evaporation
    C. act as an additional path for liquids to flow through during normal use of a plumbing fixture
    D. prevent the backflow of water in a cross-connection between a drinking water line and a sewage line

27. The designation "150 W" cast on the bonnet of a gate valve is an indication of the

    A. water working temperature
    B. water working pressure
    C. area of the opening in square inches
    D. weight of the valve in pounds

28. In the city, the size soil pipe necessary in a sewage drainage system is determined by the

    A. legal occupancy of the building
    B. vertical height of the soil line
    C. number of restrooms connected to the soil line
    D. number of "fixture units" connected to the soil line

29. Fins or other extended surfaces are used on heat exchanger tubes when

    A. the exchanger is a water-to-water exchanger
    B. water is on one side of the tube and condensing steam on the other side
    C. the surface coefficient of heat transfer on both sides of the tube is high
    D. the surface coefficient of heat transfer on one side of the tube is low compared to the coefficient on the other side of the tube

30. A fusible plug may be put in a fire tube boiler as an emergency device to indicate low water level. The fusible plug is installed so that under normal operating conditions,

    A. both sides are exposed to steam
    B. one side is exposed to water and the other side to steam
    C. one side is exposed to steam and the other side to hot gases
    D. one side is exposed to the water and the other side to hot gases

31. Extra strong wrought-iron pipe, as compared to standard wrought-iron pipe of the same nominal size, has

    A. the same outside diameter but a smaller inside diameter
    B. the same inside diameter but a larger outside diameter
    C. a larger outside diameter and a smaller inside diameter
    D. larger inside and outside diameters

32. Fans may be rated on a dynamic or a static efficiency basis. The dynamic efficiency would *probably* be

    A. lower in value because of the energy absorbed by the air velocity
    B. the same as the static in the case of centrifugal blowers running at various speeds
    C. the same as the static in the case of axial flow blowers running at various speeds
    D. higher in value than the static

33. The function of the stack relay in an oil burner installation is to

    A. regulate the draft over the fire
    B. regulate the flow of fuel oil to the burner
    C. stop the motor if the oil has not ignited
    D. stop the motor if the water or steam pressure is too high

34. The type of centrifugal pump which is inherently balanced for hydraulic thrust is the

    A. double suction impeller type
    B. single suction impeller type
    C. single stage type
    D. multistage type

35. The specifications for a job using sheet lead calls for "4-lb. sheet lead."
    This means that each sheet should weigh

    A. 4 lbs.
    B. 4 lbs. per square
    C. 4 lbs. per square foot
    D. 4 lbs. per cubic inch

36. The total cooling load design conditions for a building are divided for convenience into two components.
    These are:

    A. infiltration and radiation
    B. sensible heat and latent heat
    C. wet and dry bulb temperatures
    D. solar heat gain and moisture transfer

37. The function of a Hartford loop used on some steam boilers is to

    A. limit boiler steam pressure
    B. limit temperature of the steam
    C. prevent high water levels in the boiler
    D. prevent back flow of water from the boiler into the return main

38. Vibration from a ventilating blower can be prevented from being transmitted to the duct work by

   A. installing straighteners in the duct
   B. throttling the air supply to the blower
   C. bolting the blower tightly to the duct
   D. installing a canvas sleeve at the blower outlet

39. A specification states that access panels to suspended ceiling will be of metal. The MAIN reason for providing access panels is to

   A. improve the insulation of the ceiling
   B. improve the appearance of the ceiling
   C. make it easier to construct the building
   D. make it easier to maintain the building

40. A plumber on a job reports that the steamfitter has installed a 3" steam line in a location at which the plans show the house trap. On inspecting the job, you should

   A. tell the steamfitter to remove the steam line
   B. study the condition to see if the house trap can be relocated
   C. tell the plumber and steamfitter to work it out between themselves and then report to you
   D. tell the plumber to find another location for the trap because the steamfitter has already completed his work

41. In the installation of any heating system, the MOST important consideration is that

   A. all elements be made of a good grade of cast iron
   B. all radiators and connectors be mounted horizontally
   C. the smallest velocity of flow of heating medium be used
   D. there be proper clearance between hot surfaces and surrounding combustible material

42. Which one of the following is the PRIMARY object in drawing up a set of specifications for materials to be purchased?

   A. Control of quality
   B. Outline of intended use
   C. Establishment of standard sizes
   D. Location and method of inspection.

43. The drawing which should be used as a LEGAL reference when checking completed construction work is the _____ drawing.

   A. contract
   B. assembly
   C. working or shop
   D. preliminary

Questions 44-50.

DIRECTIONS: Questions 44 through 50 refer to the plumbing drawing shown below.

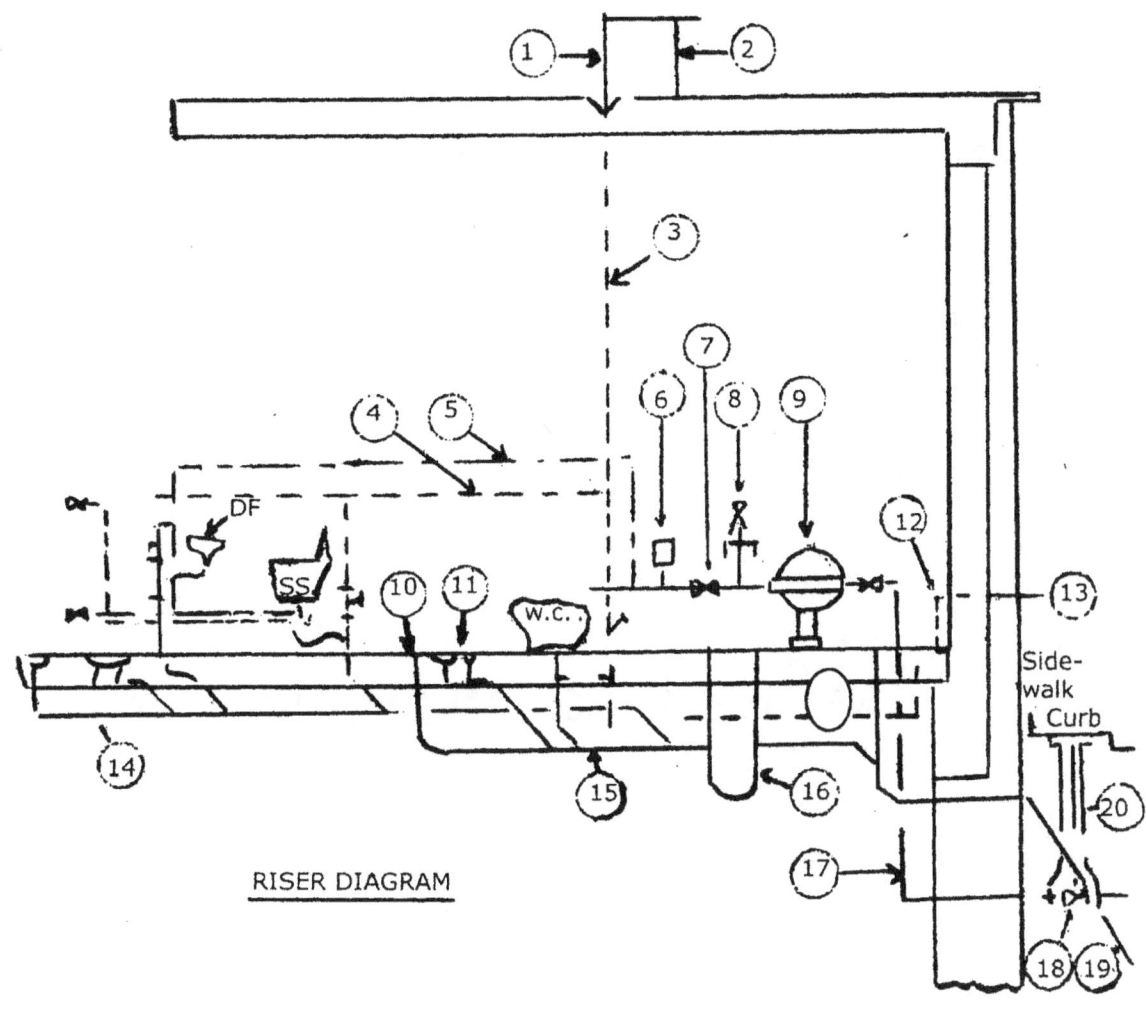

RISER DIAGRAM

44. According to the building code, the MINIMUM diameter of No. 1 and its minimum height, No. 2 respectively, are

    A. 2" and 12"
    B. 3" and 18"
    C. 4" and 24"
    D. 6" and 36"

44._____

45. No 6 is a

    A. relief valve
    B. shock absorber
    C. testing connection
    D. drain

45._____

46. No. 9 is a

    A. strainer
    B. float valve
    C. meter
    D. pedestal

46._____

47. No. 11 is a

    A. floor drain
    B. cleanout
    C. trap
    D. vent connection

47._____

48. No. ⓭ is a

   A. standpipe
   B. air inlet
   C. sprinkler head
   D. cleanout

49. The size of No. ⓰ is

   A. 2" x 2"
   B. 2" x 3"
   C. 3" x 3"
   D. 4" x 4"

50. No. ⓲ is a

   A. pressure reducing valve
   B. butterfly valve
   C. curb cock
   D. sprinkler head

KEY (CORRECT ANSWERS)

1. C	11. A	21. D	31. A	41. D
2. B	12. C	22. D	32. D	42. A
3. C	13. A	23. B	33. C	43. A
4. D	14. B	24. A	34. A	44. C
5. D	15. C	25. A	35. C	45. B
6. B	16. A	26. B	36. B	46. C
7. B	17. A	27. B	37. D	47. A
8. A	18. D	28. D	38. D	48. B
9. B	19. B	29. D	39. D	49. D
10. D	20. D	30. D	40. B	50. C

EXAMINATION SECTION
TEST 1

DIRECTIONS: Each question or incomplete statement is followed by several suggested answers or completions. Select the one that BEST answers the question or completes the statement. *PRINT THE LETTER OF THE CORRECT ANSWER IN THE SPACE AT THE RIGHT.*

1. The method used in a hand-fired furnace wherein the coal is fired on one side of the furnace while the other side is burning brightly is known as the _____ method. 1._____

    A. coking   B. spreading   C. ribbon   D. alternate

2. The measure of a fluid's resistance to flow is known as 2._____

    A. viscosity   B. hydrodynamics
    C. continuity   D. polarity

3. Demulsibility is the ability of a lubricating oil to separate from 3._____

    A. air   B. steam   C. flue gas   D. water

4. The wick in a gravity oil-feed system is generally made of 4._____

    A. rayon   B. wool   C. cotton   D. nylon

5. The temperature range to which No. 6 low sulphur fuel oil must *normally* be heated for proper atomization is _____ °F. 5._____

    A. 220-240   B. 170-200   C. 140-160   D. 120-130

6. When fuel oil is dispersed from an oil burner as a fine mist, it is said to be 6._____

    A. impelled   B. atomized
    C. crystallized   D. filtered

7. The one of the following devices that controls the fuel oil temperature leaving the oil heater is a (n) 7._____

    A. interlock   B. aquastat
    C. modutrol   D. accumulator

8. A duplex oil strainer is installed in a fuel oil line to 8._____

    A. remove impurities at twice the rate of oil flow
    B. change the direction of flow of the oil
    C. facilitate the use of various grades of oil
    D. allow uninterrupted flow of oil when one strainer is removed and cleaned

9. The oil burner *remote control switch* should generally be located 9._____

    A. on the oil burner housing
    B. at the entrance to the boiler room
    C. on a wall nearest the oil transfer pump
    D. on top of the boiler drum

10. The control that starts and stops the flow of oil to the spinning cup of a rotary cup oil burner is the

    A. magnetic oil valve
    B. transformer
    C. electrode
    D. bellows

11. Spontaneous combustion ignition is MOST likely to occur in a pile of

    A. loose planks
    B. oily tools
    C. oily rags
    D. masonite scrapings

12. Electric current is measured in units of

    A. ohms   B. amperes   C. volts   D. farads

13. A circuit breaker serves the same function as a

    A. meter   B. resistor   C. fuse   D. solenoid

14. A lead expansion anchor would normally be used to attach a bracket to a

    A. plaster ceiling
    B. masonite wall
    C. brass pipe
    D. concrete wall

15. The hardness of water is expressed in units of

    A. gpm   B. ppm   C. cop   D. stp

16. The alkaline contents of boiler feedwater can be *decreased* by

    A. blowing down the boiler
    B. adding caustic soda
    C. increasing the firing rate
    D. decreasing the speed of the feedwater pump

17. The MAJOR cause of air pollution resulting from burning fuel oil is

    A. carbon monoxide
    B. sulphur dioxide
    C. nitrogen
    D. hydrogen

18. The CO_2 content in the flue gas of an efficiently fired boiler should be approximately

    A. 30%   B. 25%   C. 15%   D. 12%

19. Of the following devices, the one which is used to determine the CO_2 content in flue gases is a(n)

    A. orsat
    B. haze gauge
    C. ammeter
    D. venturi

20. The one of the following that is known as an *actuating control* is a

    A. bellows
    B. heliostat
    C. needle valve
    D. relay

KEY (CORRECT ANSWERS)

1. D
2. A
3. D
4. B
5. B

6. B
7. B
8. D
9. B
10. A

11. C
12. B
13. C
14. D
15. B

16. A
17. B
18. D
19. A
20. D

TEST 2

DIRECTIONS: Each question or incomplete statement is followed by several suggested answers or completions. Select the one that BEST answers the question or completes the statement. *PRINT THE LETTER OF THE CORRECT ANSWER IN THE SPACE AT THE RIGHT.*

1. The function of a *pyrometer* is to measure 1._____

    A. hardness
    B. vibration
    C. polarity
    D. temperature

2. A simplex type Bourdon-tube gauge is *ordinarily* used on a steam boiler to indicate 2._____

    A. height
    B. flow
    C. temperature
    D. pressure

3. A *hydrometer* will measure 3._____

    A. specific weight
    B. viscosity
    C. specific gravity
    D. water level

4. An instrument that is used to measure gas pressure is a 4._____

    A. tachometer
    B. spectrometer
    C. potentiometer
    D. manometer

5. The packing that is *generally* used on the cold water end of a centrifugal pump is 5._____

    A. brass
    B. rubber
    C. flax
    D. graphited-asbestos

6. The one of the following wrenches that would *normally* be used on hexagonally-shaped screwed valves and fittings is the _____ wrench. 6._____

    A. open-end
    B. torque
    C. adjustable pipe
    D. hook spanner

7. A *hickey* is a device that is used to 7._____

    A. hang pipe
    B. lift heavy fittings
    C. dig a trench for a steam line
    D. bend pipe

8. A pneumatic tool is *normally* operated by 8._____

    A. propane   B. water   C. steam   D. air

9. If 50 gallons of fuel oil cost $30.00, then 60 gallons of oil at the same rate will cost 9._____

    A. $125.00   B. $90.00   C. $36.00   D. $25.00

10. Four oil burners using 50 gallons per hour operating together are to burn 100,000 gallons of No. 6 fuel oil. The number of hours that it would take to burn this quantity of oil is 10._____

    A. 500   B. 650   C. 825   D. 1,000

11. The floor area of a boiler room that is 52 feet long and 31 feet wide is _____ square feet. 11.____

    A. 1,562　　　B. 1,612　　　C. 1,721　　　D. 1,832

12. The sum of 5 1/2, 4, 3 1/4, and 2 1/2 is 12.____

    A. 15 1/4　　　B. 13 1/2　　　C. 12　　　D. 10 1/4

13. Most explosions in furnaces with oil-fired units result from *failure* to detect a 13.____

    A. dropping boiler pressure
    B. dropping steam temperature
    C. pulsating exit gas temperature
    D. loss of ignition

14. The MAIN reason why tools should NOT be left on catwalks or scaffolds is to 14.____

    A. prevent a mix-up of tools
    B. prevent the tools from being borrowed
    C. prevent damage to tools if they fell off onto the landing
    D. avoid a safety hazard

15. The proper extinguishing agent to use on a live electrical fire is 15.____

    A. carbon dioxide　　　B. steam
    C. water　　　D. foam

16. The FIRST procedure to follow upon witnessing smoke coming from an electronic control unit is to 16.____

    A. call the fire department
    B. pour water on it
    C. shut off the power
    D. look for a fire extinguisher

Questions 17-20.

DIRECTIONS: Questions 17 through 20 are to be answered SOLELY in accordance with the information contained in the following paragraph.

Steel used in boiler construction must be of a higher quality than steel used in general construction. The boiler steel must be capable of sustaining loads at elevated temperatures. Temperature has a more serious effect upon the boiler fabrication than has the pressure. The material for bolts and studs is conditioned by tempering. The tempering temperature is at least 100° F higher than the service operating temperature. All materials used in boiler construction must be creep resistant to minimize the relaxation in service. Fire box quality plate is used for any part of a boiler exposed to the fire or products of combustion. For parts of the boiler subject to pressure and not exposed to fire or products of combustion, flange quality plate is used. A small percentage of molybdenum is added to steel in the manufacture of superheater tubes, piping, and valves to increase the ability of these parts to withstand high temperature.

17. Material for bolts and studs used on boilers is conditioned for service by 17.____

    A. tempering
    B. re-tightening
    C. forging
    D. anodizing

18. The part of a boiler that is exposed to products of combustion is made of 18.____

    A. alloy materials
    B. firebox quality plate
    C. flange quality plate
    D. carbon steel

19. Temperature has a more serious effect upon boiler fabrication than has the 19.____

    A. vibration
    B. steam
    C. relaxation
    D. pressure

20. When comparing steel used in boiler construction to steel used in general construction, it can be said that steel used in boiler construction must be of a 20.____

    A. high-weld strength
    B. low-carbon content
    C. lower quality
    D. higher quality

KEY (CORRECT ANSWERS)

1.	D	11.	B
2.	D	12.	A
3.	C	13.	D
4.	D	14.	D
5.	C	15.	A
6.	A	16.	C
7.	D	17.	A
8.	D	18.	B
9.	C	19.	D
10.	A	20.	D

EXAMINATION SECTION
TEST 1

DIRECTIONS: Each question or incomplete statement is followed by several suggested answers or completions. Select the one that BEST answers the question or completes the statement. *PRINT THE LETTER OF THE CORRECT ANSWER IN THE SPACE AT THE RIGHT.*

1. An *unloader* is a device that is commonly found on a(n)

    A. steam header
    B. air compressor
    C. anemometer
    D. soot blower

2. An instrument for drawing a diagram showing actual pressure-volume relationships within the cylinder of an engine or a compressor is called a(n)

    A. barometer
    B. engine indicator
    C. pyrometer
    D. venturi meter

3. Air compressor suction and discharge valves should be cleaned with

    A. naphtha   B. benzene   C. fuel oil   D. soap suds

4. Of the following valves, the BEST one to use to restrict or throttle a flow of fluid is a _____ valve.

    A. gate
    B. quick-opening
    C. globe
    D. plug

5. The MAIN reason that try-cocks are installed on a boiler is to ensure that the

    A. boiler can be blown down
    B. water column can be blown down
    C. water gage glass is operating correctly
    D. condensate pumps are operating

6. A direct-acting duplex reciprocating steam pump is designated as 6 x 3 x 7. The numeral 6 indicates the

    A. diameter of the water cylinders
    B. length of stroke of both cylinders
    C. diameter of the steam cylinders
    D. diameter of the admission valve

7. The one of the following pumps that has NO moving parts is the _____ pump.

    A. plunger
    B. jet
    C. radial flow
    D. piston

8. Of the following types of pumps, the one which is MOST generally used to pump fuel oil is the _____ type pump.

    A. jet
    B. rotary
    C. centrifugal
    D. propeller

9. The test pressure recommended for a hydrostatic test of a boiler is _____ the working pressure.

   A. 2 1/2 times   B. 2 times   C. 1 1/2 times   D. equal to

10. Assume that a boiler has been out of service for repairs and is now ready to be put back on the line.
    Of the following, the FIRST step operating personnel should take is to

    A. fill the boiler with water
    B. open the vents
    C. blow boiler tubes
    D. inspect the inside and outside of the boiler

11. The one of the following that is a water-tube boiler is the _____ boiler.

    A. horizontal return tubular
    B. bent-tube
    C. economic
    D. horizontal two-pass

12. An oil-fired high pressure boiler has to be taken off the line.
    Of the following procedures, the FIRST step would be to

    A. reduce the fuel feed and slowly decrease the output
    B. manually close the non-return valve
    C. open the drain connections between the non-return and the head stop valve
    D. close the feedwater-supply valve

13. A drop in steam pressure, as indicated by the steam gauge, of a normally operating steam boiler would MOST likely indicate that the

    A. fuel supply must be increased
    B. boiler must be blown down
    C. speed of the feedwater pump must be increased
    D. low water cut-off is inoperative

14. Steam that has been heated above the temperature corresponding to its pressure is said to be

    A. superheated   B. pressurized
    C. tempered   D. overheated

15. In a shutdown of a boiler to prevent the creation of a vacuum from the condensing steam within the boiler, the steam drum vent valve should be opened when the steam pressure has dropped to approximately _____ psi.

    A. 100   B. 75   C. 50   D. 25

16. An attemperator is a device used to control or regulate

    A. air temperature   B. steam temperature
    C. oil pressure   D. water pressure

17. The number of safety valves on the boiler drum of a power boiler with a heating surface of 500 square feet is AT LEAST

    A. 2   B. 3   C. 4   D. 5

18. The fusible plug of an HRT boiler is located in the

    A. hot water tank
    B. rear head
    C. fire door
    D. water column

19. Boiler tube size is designated by its

    A. boiler location
    B. wall thickness
    C. external diameter
    D. internal diameter

20. A feedwater heater is installed in a steam generating system PRIMARILY to

    A. furnish hot water to the building
    B. generate hot feedwater for the building radiators
    C. condition and heat feedwater to the boiler
    D. distribute high pressure steam

KEY (CORRECT ANSWERS)

1.	B	11.	B
2.	B	12.	A
3.	D	13.	A
4.	C	14.	A
5.	C	15.	D
6.	C	16.	B
7.	B	17.	A
8.	B	18.	B
9.	C	19.	C
10.	D	20.	C

TEST 2

DIRECTIONS: Each question or incomplete statement is followed by several suggested answers or completions. Select the one that BEST answers the question or completes the statement. *PRINT THE LETTER OF THE CORRECT ANSWER IN THE SPACE AT THE RIGHT.*

1. A balanced draft in a boiler consists of

   A. a forced draft fan only
   B. a natural chimney draft only
   C. both forced and induced draft
   D. both induced and natural draft

2. One horsepower is *electrically equivalent* to 746

   A. watts   B. calories   C. joules   D. kilowatts

3. Of the following pH values, the one which indicates that a solution is *neither* acid *nor* alkaline is

   A. 3   B. 4   C. 7   D. 10

4. Zinc bars are sometimes placed in boilers to

   A. increase the pH value of the feedwater
   B. eliminate foul gases in the steam
   C. prevent corrosion
   D. decrease foaming and priming

5. The MAIN function of an evaporator is to remove impurities in

   A. air   B. oil   C. water   D. grease

6. The MAIN reason why a caustic boil-out of a boiler would be necessary is that the boiler has accumulated a deposit of

   A. sediment   B. oil   C. scale   D. slime

7. Of the following, the type of steam traps that does NOT have any moving parts is the

   A. inverted bucket   B. impulse
   C. continuous-flow   D. float-actuated

8. The one of the following valves that permits fluid to flow in one direction only is the

   A. check   B. plug   C. globe   D. stop

9. A 1/2 inch diameter galvanized pipe that is 3" long and has male threads at both ends is known as a

   A. tube   B. flange   C. joint   D. nipple

10. The one of the following pipe fittings that should be used to connect a 1 1/2"-diameter pipe is a(n)

    A. saddle   B. increaser   C. elbow   D. nipple

32

11. A receiver in a compressed air system

    A. stores lubricating oil
    B. stores compressed air
    C. furnishes air to the air compressor
    D. acts as a pressure relief

12. The device that stops or starts a fully automatic oil burner at a predetermined pressure is called a

    A. hydrostat
    B. thermostat
    C. pressuretrol
    D. transformer

13. Of the following statements, the one which is CORRECT as pertains to a closed-type feedwater heater is that the

    A. steam and water mix
    B. water will be heated to within a few degrees of the steam temperature
    C. feedwater heater is located at an elevation above the boiler feed pump
    D. floating impurities are removed from the surface of the water through the overflow weir

14. The function of *cooling towers* is to

    A. cool condenser water
    B. supply drinking water
    C. cool the boiler room
    D. circulate the boiler feedwater

15. The function of an oil separator in a non-condensing steam plant is to remove oil from

    A. exhaust steam
    B. compressed air
    C. feedwater
    D. liquid ammonia

16. An economizer is generally located between the

    A. feedwater heater and feed pump
    B. air compressor and receiver
    C. suction and discharge oil strainers
    D. boiler and the stack

17. Of the following types of equipment used to remove fly ash from flue gases, the one which is the MOST commonly installed in commercial boilers is the

    A. electrostatic precipitator
    B. mechanical collector
    C. fabric filter
    D. wet scrubber

18. The one of the following general classes of stokers in which coal is admitted below the point of air admission is the _____ stoker.

    A. underfeed
    B. chain grate
    C. traveling grate
    D. spreader

19. The fuel bed of an underfeed stoker has the green coal at the

    A. bottom
    B. top
    C. middle
    D. burning surface

20. The one of the following coals that has a restriction on its use in New York City is

    A. canel
    B. lignite
    C. bituminous
    D. anthracite

KEY (CORRECT ANSWERS)

1.	C	11.	B
2.	A	12.	C
3.	C	13.	B
4.	C	14.	A
5.	C	15.	A
6.	B	16.	D
7.	C	17.	A
8.	A	18.	A
9.	D	19.	A
10.	B	20.	C

EXAMINATION SECTION
TEST 1

DIRECTIONS: Each question or incomplete statement is followed by several suggested answers or completions. Select the one that BEST answers the question or completes the statement. *PRINT THE LETTER OF THE CORRECT ANSWER IN THE SPACE AT THE RIGHT.*

1. The temperature at which water in an open vessel at sea level will boil is MOST NEARLY   1._____

    A. 100° F   B. 180° F   C. 212° F   D. 300° F

2. The fraction 3/8, expressed as a decimal, is   2._____

    A. 0.250   B. 0.281   C. 0.375   D. 0.406

3. The process of removing water, dissolved solids, and sludge from a boiler is called   3._____

    A. blowing down   B. screening
    C. topping   D. feeding

4. The remote control switch for all of the oil burners in a boiler room should be located   4._____

    A. adjacent to the boiler
    B. at each entrance to the boiler room
    C. on the mezzanine of the boiler room
    D. on the side of the boiler nearest an exit door

5. Of the following, an electrical fire should be extinguished with a fire extinguisher containing   5._____

    A. carbon tetrachloride   B. foamite
    C. carbon dioxide   D. soda acid

6. A steam preheater is COMMONLY used to   6._____

    A. generate superheated steam
    B. heat boiler make-up water
    C. heat #6 fuel oil before burning
    D. heat atmospheric air prior to combustion

7. Atomization as it applies to boiler operation is the process of   7._____

    A. breaking up atoms to obtain nuclear energy
    B. breaking up fuel oil into fine particles
    C. vaporizing water into steam
    D. mixing air and steam

8. The purpose of the try-cocks on a boiler is PRIMARILY to   8._____

    A. drain water from the boiler
    B. check the gage glass reading
    C. drain water from the gage glass
    D. blow down the boiler

9. A receiver in a compressed air system is used PRIMARILY to

   A. cool the air
   B. store the air
   C. remove particles of dust from the air
   D. saturate the air with vapor

10. A gage that can be used to measure either positive pressure or vacuum is GENERALLY called a _____ gage.

    A. pump   B. sight   C. compound   D. steam

11. With respect to heating systems, the MAIN purpose of using a thermostat in a room is to

    A. improve the efficiency of the oil burner
    B. increase the flow of heated air
    C. regulate the humidity
    D. regulate the temperature

12. An inter-cooler is a device USUALLY used on a

    A. refrigerator
    B. rotary gear pump
    C. centrifugal pump
    D. multistage air compressor

13. A boiler feed water regulator automatically regulates the _____ the boiler.

    A. supply of make-up water to
    B. temperature of the water being supplied to
    C. maximum water temperature in
    D. pressure of the water being supplied to

14. In the electrical trade, the term BX refers to

    A. amplifier hook-up wires
    B. insulated wires in a rigid conduit
    C. a cable consisting of insulated wires in a flexible metal tubing
    D. a cable consisting of insulated wires in a plastic outer covering

15. When threading pipe, the tool that holds the die is called a

    A. holder   B. stock   C. yawl   D. wedge

16. The PROPER tool to use to remove the burrs from the inside of a pipe is a

    A. chisel   B. file   C. cutter   D. reamer

17. The wrench which is MOST often used to make connections in the piping for a boiler is a

    A. pump pliers   B. gas pliers
    C. Stillson wrench   D. vise-grip pliers

18. If the combustion sensing device (lead sulphide cell) in a boiler installation does not *see* a flame, the boiler is automatically shut down by the closing of the

    A. breech damper
    B. magnetic oil valve
    C. primary air supply damper
    D. secondary air supply damper

19. A wrench that is COMMONLY used to tighten a nut where only a short swing of the wrench handle is possible is called a(n) _____ wrench.

    A. Stillson   B. monkey   C. ratchet   D. allen

20. A solenoid valve is GENERALLY operated by

    A. water temperature   B. water pressure
    C. electricity   D. oil pressure

21. The water hammer noise that is sometimes heard in the steam lines of a heating system is USUALLY caused by

    A. high steam pressure
    B. condensation in the steam
    C. impurities in the boiler water
    D. high flue gas temperatures

22. A sump system in a building is NORMALLY used to collect all boiler room waste water and move it into the house

    A. transfer pump   B. settling tank
    C. sewer   D. recirculation tank

23. A centrifugal pump is located above a sump pit. The type of valve that is installed on the end of the suction line to the pump to assure that the line is primed is called a _____ valve.

    A. needle   B. gate   C. globe   D. foot

24. A gag or clamp on a safety valve is GENERALLY used when

    A. making a hydrostatic test on a boiler
    B. testing the setting of the safety valve
    C. filling the boiler with water
    D. testing the quality of the water

25. The PRIME function of an electrical circuit breaker is similar to that of a

    A. capacitor   B. conductance
    C. switch   D. fuse

26. A valve that opens when a solenoid is energized and closes when it is de-energized is called a _____ valve.

    A. thermistor   B. magnetic
    C. thermostatic   D. pressure regulator

27. The device which stops the flow of fuel oil to an oil burner in case of primary air failure is GENERALLY known as a

   A. thermostat
   B. vaporstat
   C. pressuretrol
   D. low pressure cut-off

28. A device that is used to start the operation of high voltage electrical equipment by means of a low voltage control circuit is called a

   A. relay
   B. Wheatstone bridge
   C. Hartley circuit
   D. thermocouple

29. A pyrometer can be used to measure the

   A. temperature of flue gas
   B. pressure of fuel oil
   C. percentage of CO_2 in flue gas
   D. amount of soot in flue gas

30. The low water cut-off in a boiler is USUALLY controlled by means of a

   A. bimetallic strip
   B. float
   C. relay
   D. bellows

31. The type of pump COMMONLY used to pump No. 6 fuel oil from the storage oil tanks is a(n) _____ pump.

   A. centrifugal
   B. reciprocating
   C. gear
   D. axial

32. One of the uses of a pressuretrol on a fuel oil fired steam boiler is to

   A. control the water pressure so that it is equal to the steam pressure
   B. prevent the steam pressure from exceeding a set value
   C. control the pressure of the fuel oil so that it does not exceed the relief valve setting
   D. control the pressure of the condensate to the vacuum pump

33. The GREATEST safety hazard of storing oily rags is that they can

   A. cause a fire
   B. cause a foul odor
   C. produce toxic fumes
   D. attract vermin

34. Of the following, the BEST action to take if you find a small puddle of oil on the boiler room floor is to

   A. ignore it
   B. mop it up
   C. tell your supervisor
   D. cover it with sawdust

35. When a long ladder is placed against a high wall, a rope should be tied from the lowest rung to the wall.
   This is done to prevent

   A. anyone from walking under the ladder
   B. the ladder from slipping
   C. the rungs of the ladder from breaking
   D. someone from removing the ladder

36. Your fellow worker lifts one end of a piece of heavy equipment with a crowbar to permit you to work under this equipment with your hands.
    The PROPER safe procedure that you should follow is to

    A. insert temporary support blocks
    B. complete the job rapidly
    C. use heavy leather gloves
    D. lash the handle of the crowbar

37. Regulations require that domestic hot water should be supplied between the hours of

    A. 6:00 A.M. to 6:00 P.M.
    B. 6:00 A.M. to 12:00 Midnight
    C. 8:00 A.M. to 10:00 P.M.
    D. 12:00 Noon to 12:00 Midnight

38. In a fire tube boiler, it is MOST important to remove the soot from the

    A. outside surface of the tubes
    B. inside surface of the tubes
    C. walls of the combustion chamber
    D. intermediate tube sheet

39. A steam heating boiler is classified as a low pressure boiler when it generates steam at a gage pressure

    A. between 50 and 70 pounds per square inch
    B. between 30 and 50 pounds per square inch
    C. of 30 pounds per square inch or less
    D. of 15 pounds per square inch or less

40. The safety valve which is found on a steam boiler is designed to prevent the _____ from becoming too high.

    A. stack temperature
    B. water level
    C. steam pressure
    D. oil supply pressure

KEY (CORRECT ANSWERS)

1. C	11. D	21. B	31. C
2. C	12. D	22. C	32. B
3. A	13. A	23. D	33. A
4. B	14. C	24. A	34. B
5. C	15. B	25. D	35. B
6. C	16. D	26. B	36. A
7. B	17. C	27. B	37. B
8. B	18. B	28. A	38. B
9. B	19. C	29. A	39. D
10. C	20. C	30. B	40. C

TEST 2

DIRECTIONS: Each question or incomplete statement is followed by several suggested answers or completions. Select the one that BEST answers the question or completes the statement. *PRINT THE LETTER OF THE CORRECT ANSWER IN THE SPACE AT THE RIGHT.*

1. From the standpoint of corrosion resistance and reliability, the PREFERRED material for domestic hot water pipes from among the following is 1._____

    A. lead   B. brass   C. steel   D. plastic

2. The packing which is GENERALLY found in the stuffing box of a centrifugal water pump is used to 2._____

    A. reduce bearing wear
    B. reduce noise
    C. prevent leakage of water
    D. compensate for shaft misalignment

3. The MAIN function of a steam trap is to 3._____

    A. remove condensate from a steam supply line
    B. restrict the flow of steam in a supply line
    C. filter dirt out of a condensate return line
    D. remove steam from a water line

4. The sum of 2'6", 0'3", and 3'1" is 4._____

    A. 2'9"   B. 5'7"   C. 5'10"   D. 15'0"

5. A union is a plumbing fitting that is MOST commonly used to join 5._____

    A. two pieces of threaded pipe of the same diameter
    B. two pieces of threaded pipe of different diameter
    C. a gate valve to a threaded pipe
    D. an angle valve to a gate valve

6. A drain valve is used on a compressed air tank for the purpose of 6._____

    A. protecting the tank against excessively high pressures
    B. removing condensed vapor from the tank
    C. preventing air leakage from the tank
    D. starting the compressor

7. A valve which permits fluid to flow only in one direction in a pipe is called a _____ valve. 7._____

    A. needle   B. gate   C. globe   D. check

8. The shade or color of the smoke emitted from burning fuel oil in a burner can be compared to a standard chart called a _____ chart. 8._____

    A. Neumann   B. Ringelmann
    C. Mann   D. Kirchoff

40

9. The three MOST important pollutants which come from burning fuel oil are: particulates, carbon monoxide, and

   A. oxygen
   B. carbon dioxide
   C. sulphur dioxide
   D. nitrogen

10. Number 6 fuel oil must be preheated before burning to

    A. reduce its viscosity
    B. increase its viscosity
    C. make use of excess steam
    D. make use of excess electricity

11. The deposits on the rotary oil cup of a burner should be cleaned with

    A. a file
    B. a metal scraper
    C. kerosene and a rag
    D. emery cloth

12. The low-water cut-off on a boiler should be tested by

    A. *lowering* the water level slowly
    B. *raising* the water level slowly
    C. *increasing* the firing rate
    D. *lowering* the firing rate

13. One POSSIBLE cause of smoke from an oil-fired boiler is

    A. contaminated boiler water
    B. low setting of the boiler relief valve
    C. low level of water in the boiler
    D. cold oil

14. The combustion efficiency of an oil-fired boiler can be determined from a combination of the _____ temperature and the percentage of _____ in the flue gas.

    A. flue gas; oxygen
    B. flue gas; carbon dioxide
    C. steam; oxygen
    D. steam; carbon monoxide

15. A relief valve is usually placed on the discharge side of the positive displacement fuel oil pump used to pump oil from the tank to the burner.
    The MAIN purpose of this relief valve is to

    A. increase the flow of oil to the burner
    B. increase the temperature of the fuel oil
    C. remove entrapped air
    D. protect the oil pump

16. To insure proper burning, the No. 6 fuel oil going to the oil burner is heated to a temperature that is MOST NEARLY

    A. 220° F   B. 180° F   C. 140° F   D. 100° F

17. The device that regulates the amount of steam flowing through a fuel oil steam preheater is called a

A. fuel oil pressure valve
B. fuel oil volume flow meter
C. steam volume flow meter
D. steam temperature regulator valve

18. Of the following materials, the one that is considered to have the BEST heat insulation property for a given thickness is

   A. wood
   B. glass wool
   C. copper
   D. steel

19. The function of the modutrol motor on a boiler is to

   A. open and close the fuel oil metering valve at the oil burner
   B. open and close the flow of fuel oil to the fuel oil heater
   C. control the flow of fuel oil from the storage tank
   D. control the flow of gas to ignite the fuel

20. The ignition system for an oil burner that burns No. 6 oil NORMALLY consists of a transformer, insulated electrodes and a(n)

   A. magnetic gas valve
   B. oil valve
   C. thermometer
   D. flow meter

21. A combustion sensing device, such as a lead sulfide cell, will close the magnetic valve feeding oil to the burner if it does not see a flame in APPROXIMATELY _____ to _____ seconds.

   A. $1; 1\frac{1}{2}$
   B. $2; 4$
   C. $4\frac{1}{2}; 6$
   D. $8; 16$

22. Bimetallic elements are NORMALLY found in _____ devices.

   A. pressure control
   B. temperature control
   C. pressure relief
   D. water level control

23. The cold oil interlock which prevents the oil burner from starting if the oil is too cold for proper smoke-free operation is located in the

   A. oil tank
   B. oil burner
   C. oil pump
   D. electric oil heater

24. The air flow interlock which will prevent the fuel oil valve from opening if there is no air pressure is located

   A. in the oil cup
   B. on top of the fan casing
   C. in the flue stack
   D. in the combustion chamber

25. A dirty or damaged oil cup in a rotary cup burner is MOST likely to cause

   A. poor mixing of oil and air
   B. an increase in oil flow
   C. an increase in oil pressure
   D. a decrease in air flow

26. The burner and boiler should each be inspected, cleaned, and overhauled _____ year(s).

    A. at least once a
    B. once every two
    C. once every three
    D. once every five

27. The accuracy of a fuel oil tank capacity gage is checked with a

    A. weighing scale
    B. pressure gage
    C. density meter
    D. dip stick

28. Vacuum tubes in oil burner control devices must be replaced even if they are in operating condition once every _____ months.

    A. 3 B. 6 C. 12 D. 18

29. The soot blower used to blow soot out of the boiler tubes must be operated ONLY

    A. when the oil burner is shut down for at least 30 minutes
    B. when the oil burner is in operation
    C. when the oil burner is removed
    D. prior to operation of the burner

30. The pipe that leads from the storage oil tank to the outside of the building and which is at least 2 feet above the curb line and open to the atmosphere is called a _____ line.

    A. vent
    B. fill
    C. oil depth check
    D. suction

31. The device used to regulate draft in a furnace is called a

    A. damper B. stay bolt C. bonnet D. mudring

32. The secondary air damper is located under the burner, and the APPROXIMATE percentage of the total air that this damper supplies for complete fuel combustion is

    A. 30% B. 45% C. 70% D. 85%

33. The color that is MOST commonly used to identify a fire standpipe is

    A. bright red
    B. black
    C. bright blue
    D. silver gray

34. The device that starts and stops the sump pump at predetermined water levels in the sump pit is called a _____ switch.

    A. float
    B. micro
    C. double pole
    D. single pole

Questions 35-40.

DIRECTIONS: Questions 35 through 40, inclusive, are based on the paragraph *Hot Water Generation* shown below. When answering these questions, refer ONLY to this paragraph.

HOT WATER GENERATION

The hot water that comes from a faucet is called Domestic Hot Water.

It is heated by a steam coil that runs through a storage tank full of water in the basement of each building.

As the tenants take the hot water, fresh cold water enters the tank and is heated. The temperature of this water is automatically kept at approximately 140° F.

The device which controls the temperature is called a temperature regulator valve. It is operated by a bellows, capillary tube, and thermo bulb which connects between the valve and the hot water being stored in the tank. This bulb, tube, and bellows contains a liquid which expands and contracts with changes in temperature.

As the water in the tank reaches 140° F, the liquid in the thermo bulb expands and causes pressure to travel along the capillary tube and into the bellows. The expanded liquid forces the bellows to push the Temperature Regulator Valve Stem down, closing the valve. No more steam can enter the coil in the tank, and the water will get no hotter.

As the hot water is used by the tenants, cold water enters the tank and pulls the temperature down. This causes the liquid in the thermo bulb to cool and contract (shrink). The pressure is no longer in the bellows and a spring pushes it up, allowing the valve to open and allowing steam to again enter the heating coil in the storage tank raising the temperature of the Domestic Hot Water to 140° F.

35. Domestic hot water is heated by

   A. coal
   B. electricity
   C. hot water
   D. steam

36. The temperature of domestic hot water is MOST NEARLY

   A. 75° F
   B. 100° F
   C. 140° F
   D. 212° F

37. The temperature of the hot water is controlled by a

   A. thermometer
   B. temperature regulator valve
   C. pressuretrol
   D. pressure gauge

38. The temperature regulator valve is operated by a combination of a

   A. thermometer and a thermo bulb
   B. thermometer and a pyrometer
   C. bellows, capillary tube, and a thermometer
   D. bellows, capillary tube, and a thermo bulb

39. Closing of the temperature regulator valve prevents _____ from entering the heating coil in the tank.

   A. water
   B. steam
   C. electricity
   D. air

40. As hot water is used by the tenants, the temperature of the water in the tank 40.____

    A. increases
    B. decreases
    C. remains the same
    D. approaches 212° F

KEY (CORRECT ANSWERS)

1. B	11. C	21. B	31. A
2. C	12. A	22. B	32. D
3. A	13. D	23. D	33. A
4. C	14. B	24. B	34. A
5. A	15. D	25. A	35. D
6. B	16. B	26. A	36. C
7. D	17. D	27. D	37. B
8. B	18. B	28. C	38. D
9. C	19. A	29. B	39. B
10. A	20. A	30. A	40. B

EXAMINATION SECTION
TEST 1

DIRECTIONS: Each question or incomplete statement is followed by several suggested answers or completions. Select the one that BEST answers the question or completes the statement. *PRINT THE LETTER OF THE CORRECT ANSWER IN THE SPACE AT THE RIGHT.*

1. Of the following classifications of fuel oils, the one which is NO longer made is 1.____

   A. #1 B. #2 C. #3 D. #6

2. Water at sea level and atmospheric pressure in an open container will boil at a temperature of 2.____

   A. 238° F B. 212° F C. 190° F D. 172° F

3. A gauge pressure of 6.1 psi is equivalent to an absolute pressure of MOST NEARLY _____ psia. 3.____

   A. 30 B. 26 C. 21 D. 16

4. A pyrometer is used to measure 4.____

   A. draft B. resistance
   C. temperature D. velocity

5. Furnace draft is USUALLY measured in 5.____

   A. cubic feet B. feet of mercury
   C. inches of air D. inches of water

6. An ORSAT apparatus is used in a boiler plant to analyze 6.____

   A. feedwater B. flue gas
   C. fuel D. smoke haze

7. The device that prevents explosions in oil-fired boilers due to flame failure is the 7.____

   A. mercury tube B. light sensing unit
   C. electrical transformer D. limit switch

8. The water level in a boiler operating 24 hours a day should be checked 8.____

   A. every 8 hours B. once every 16 hours
   C. weekly D. once every month

9. The boiler and oil burner should be inspected, overhauled, and cleaned at least once every 9.____

   A. 3 years B. 18 months
   C. year D. month

10. The PROPER procedure to follow when taking a boiler out of service is to 10.____

    A. *reduce* the fuel feed and slowly decrease the output
    B. *increase* the fuel feed and open all dampers

47

C. *open* all water supply valves and drain the boiler
D. *increase* the steam pressure and burn all the fuel

11. In the city, health regulations require domestic hot water to be supplied to tenants only between the hours of

    A. 6:00 A.M. to 12:00 Midnight
    B. 8:00 A.M. to 8:00 P.M.
    C. 12:00 Noon to 12:00 Midnight
    D. 10:00 A.M. to 6:00 P.M.

12. In an efficiently operated heating plant, the flue gas temperature should be APPROXIMATELY

    A. 150° F   B. 200° F   C. 350° F   D. 800° F

13. For MAXIMUM heat efficiency in a fire tube boiler, soot must be removed from the

    A. lifting rings
    B. outer tube surfaces
    C. walls of the crown sheet
    D. inner surface of the tubes

14. The percentage of carbon dioxide in the flue gas of an efficiently operated boiler should be APPROXIMATELY

    A. 4%   B. 6%   C. 12%   D. 18%

15. The combustion efficiency of a boiler is indicated by the amount of carbon dioxide in the flue gas and the

    A. size of the stack
    B. quality of the fuel
    C. temperature of the combustion air
    D. temperature of the flue gas

16. The pH value of boiler feedwater is normally MOST NEARLY kept at

    A. 3   B. 6   C. 10   D. 13

17. The one of the following that is used in the internal treatment of boiler feedwater to increase alkalinity is

    A. oxygen   B. tannin
    C. sodium alginate   D. soda ash

18. Of the following types of pumps, the one that is MOST commonly used with gun-type oil burners is the

    A. external or internal gear pump
    B. volute type
    C. centrifugal type
    D. propeller type

19. The hole in a direct-contact fire-actuated plug as used in a boiler is USUALLY filled with   19.____

   A. brass   B. lead   C. carbon   D. tin

20. The MAIN reason why soot blowers must be used only when the oil burners are in operation is to   20.____

   A. prevent a possible explosion
   B. reduce air pollution
   C. maintain building temperatures
   D. increase the boiler water temperature

21. The boiler low water cut-off is controlled by a   21.____

   A. relay   B. float   C. diaphragm   D. spring

22. The boiler connection from the last pass to the breech is called the   22.____

   A. drypan   B. rear tube
   C. safety outlet   D. bonnet

23. The function of a condensation pump in a steam system is to   23.____

   A. direct condensate to the house sewer
   B. prime the boiler
   C. condense steam to water
   D. return hot condensate to the boiler

24. A steam heating system that operates under both vacuum and low pressure conditions without the use of a vacuum pump is called a(n) _____ system.   24.____

   A. air   B. vapor   C. vacuum   D. water

25. A hot water heating boiler is classified as a low pressure boiler when it makes hot water at a gauge pressure NOT more than _____ psi.   25.____

   A. 300   B. 260   C. 200   D. 160

26. The one of the following gauge pressures that is MOST characteristic of a low pressure steam boiler is _____ psi.   26.____

   A. 30   B. 25   C. 20   D. 10

27. In the event of low water in a boiler, the burner will be shut down by the   27.____

   A. ignition transformer
   B. low water cut-off
   C. centrifugal switch on the burner
   D. damper control

28. A fuel oil steam preheater is USUALLY equipped with a   28.____

   A. mudring device
   B. steam temperature regulating valve
   C. steam volume gage
   D. boiler water level indicator

29. The MAIN function of a steam trap in a boiler heating system is to

    A. collect sediment from the steam lines
    B. return heat from the hot water to the building
    C. lower the temperature of the steam
    D. collect the water of condensation from steam apparatus

30. The one of the following which is a device that prevents the steam pressure in an oil-fired boiler from rising above a specified value is the

    A. pressuretrol
    B. magnetic oil valve
    C. haze gauge
    D. vaporstat

31. The type of valve used in feedwater lines where flow in only one direction is required is

    A. stop   B. gate   C. plug   D. check

32. The device that is used to force water into a boiler operating under pressure is the

    A. duplex
    B. slide valve
    C. rocker arm
    D. injector

33. The function of a feedwater heater in a boiler plant is to

    A. generate hot water for the building
    B. regulate the hot water temperature
    C. heat and condition water for the boiler
    D. condition chemicals for water leaving the boiler

34. A hot water heating system has an expansion tank to compensate for changes in the

    A. volume of water in the system
    B. volume of steam in the system
    C. water treatment process
    D. piping runs due to expansion of the metal pipe

35. One gallon of potable water weighs APPROXIMATELY _____ lbs.

    A. 6.8   B. 7.5   C. 8.3   D. 9.6

36. The bridge wall in a heating boiler is located

    A. above the arch
    B. in the steam drum
    C. behind the grates
    D. at the base of the chimney

37. A clamp or gag on a safety valve is generally used ONLY when

    A. testing a boiler hydrostatically
    B. surface-blowing the boiler
    C. adding chemicals to the feedwater
    D. cleaning the oil burner

38. Make-up water to a boiler is automatically controlled by the

   A. boiler water temperature
   B. boiler pressure
   C. metering valve
   D. feedwater regulator

39. Try-cocks are installed on a boiler for

   A. relieving air pressure in the system
   B. indicating the water level in the boiler
   C. blowing out the excess water from the boiler
   D. draining the water column

40. Steam preheaters are USUALLY used in an oil burning installation to

   A. preheat boiler feedwater
   B. add heat to saturated steam
   C. raise the temperature of the flue gas
   D. heat the fuel oil before it enters the burner

KEY (CORRECT ANSWERS)

1. C	11. A	21. B	31. D
2. B	12. C	22. D	32. D
3. C	13. D	23. D	33. C
4. C	14. C	24. B	34. A
5. D	15. D	25. D	35. C
6. B	16. C	26. D	36. C
7. B	17. D	27. B	37. A
8. A	18. A	28. B	38. D
9. C	19. D	29. D	39. B
10. A	20. A	30. A	40. D

TEST 2

DIRECTIONS: Each question or incomplete statement is followed by several suggested answers or completions. Select the one that BEST answers the question or completes the statement. *PRINT THE LETTER OF THE CORRECT ANSWER IN THE SPACE AT THE RIGHT.*

1. The temperature in a heated room can be regulated by a

   A. trap   B. scanner   C. damper   D. thermostat

   1.____

2. Impurities and solids are removed from boiler water by a procedure known as

   A. screening B. blowing down
   C. priming   D. foaming

   2.____

3. To throttle the flow of steam in a steam line, use a

   A. brass mounting B. gate valve
   C. globe valve   D. union

   3.____

4. A highly objectionable air pollutant of fuel oil is

   A. nitrogen   B. carbon   C. hydrogen   D. sulphur

   4.____

5. The modutrol motor on an oil-fired boiler controls the

   A. primary air damper
   B. gas flow for ignition
   C. oil returning to the fuel tank
   D. safety gauge

   5.____

6. The one of the following that stops the flow of oil to the spinning cup of a rotary cup oil burner is the

   A. metering valve   B. magnetic oil valve
   C. regulating valve D. fan casing

   6.____

7. The one of the following that stops the flow of fuel oil to a rotary cup oil burner in the event of primary air failure is the

   A. vaporstat   B. electrode
   C. primary air damper D. gas stop valve

   7.____

8. In a rotary cup oil burner, the breaking up of the fuel oil into fine droplets is known as

   A. aeration   B. vaporization
   C. atomization D. injection

   8.____

9. The one of the following devices that controls the fuel oil temperature leaving the oil heater is the

   A. oil interlock B. strainer
   C. aquastat   D. suction valve

   9.____

52

10. Of the following causes of smoke in oil-burning installations, the one which occurs MOST frequently is

    A. faulty atomization due to insufficient preheat
    B. insufficient draft loss through the boiler
    C. insufficient air due to lack of draft
    D. too much oil being fed into a cold furnace on starting

11. The stack switch shuts off the oil to an oil burner in the event of

    A. an air pollution alert
    B. excessive boiler pressures
    C. on oversupply of fuel
    D. flame failure

12. In the city, the Ringelmann Chart is used to determine the density of

    A. smoke   B. coal   C. fuel oil   D. water

13. A centrifugal pump is MAINLY packed to

    A. prevent water leakage   B. lubricate the bearings
    C. reduce heat   D. prevent noise

14. The BEST procedure to follow when lubricating a pump is to apply lubricant

    A. only if needed
    B. on a regular schedule
    C. whenever you think the lubricant is low
    D. only when the pump is shut down

15. When pumping water out of a pit, the one of the following that should be installed on the suction end of the line is a

    A. foot valve   B. throttle valve
    C. volute   D. governor

16. The ASME Boiler Code is used for rating boilers. The letters ASME are an abbreviation for

    A. Allied for Standards of Mechanical Engineers
    B. American Society of Mechanical Engineers
    C. American Steam Maintenance Engineers
    D. American Society of Methods Engineers

17. The function of a sump pump in a boiler room is to collect boiler room drips and discharge it into the

    A. transfer tank   B. nearest public street
    C. conditioning tank   D. house sewer

18. Of the following instruments, the one that is used to measure atmospheric pressure is a(n)

    A. odometer   B. thermometer
    C. barometer   D. manometer

19. A compound gauge measures
    A. humidity and vacuum
    B. temperature and pressure
    C. pressure and vibration
    D. pressure and vacuum

20. An inter-cooler would GENERALLY be installed on a(n)
    A. air compressor
    B. rotary gear pump
    C. fuel tank
    D. evaporator

21. The one of the following that is BEST to use to loosen a rusted bolt is
    A. penetrating oil
    B. engine oil
    C. graphite
    D. silica

22. The one of the following that is used to thread a pipe externally is called a
    A. guide   B. die   C. stock   D. tap

23. A frequent cause of knocking in low-pressure steam lines is
    A. condensation of the steam
    B. an increase of steam temperature
    C. high water temperature
    D. insufficient fuel supply

24. Viscosity is a measure of the resistance of a fuel oil to
    A. burning
    B. flowing
    C. vaporization
    D. deterioration

25. The PROPER procedure to follow for safety when working on a ladder is to
    A. not face the ladder when descending
    B. use a sturdy object to obtain additional ladder height
    C. take one step at a time when ascending or descending a ladder
    D. always have two men on the ladder at the same time

26. Oily waste rags should be kept in a closed metal container MAINLY to
    A. prevent fire
    B. keep the rags from drying out
    C. eliminate attraction to bugs
    D. prevent oil seepage onto the floor

27. Fire standpipe systems are GENERALLY painted
    A. black   B. red   C. blue   D. white

28. The oil burner remote control switch should be located
    A. on the front of the boiler
    B. on the stack of the boiler
    C. at the control panel
    D. at each entrance to the boiler room

29. Insulated electrical wire in flexible metal tubing is known as

   A. BX   B. cable   C. RX   D. conduit

30. The one of the following that is used to measure air pressure is a

   A. calorimeter   B. venturi
   C. compensator   D. manometer

31. Pressures below atmospheric are USUALLY expressed in

   A. pounds of air   B. inches of water
   C. inches of mercury   D. pounds of steam

32. The reading of the fuel oil tank capacity gauge is checked by using a

   A. steam nozzle   B. dip stick
   C. drip pan   D. pressure gauge

33. In piping systems, nominal size refers to

   A. outside diameter   B. length in feet
   C. inside diameter   D. weight in pounds

34. The one of the following plumbing fittings which is used to connect two pieces of the same diameter threaded pipe is a

   A. cap   B. bushing   C. union   D. plug

35. A four-inch-long galvanized pipe having a diameter of one inch and male threads at both ends is called a(n)

   A. nipple   B. turnbuckle
   C. elbow   D. coupling

36. A galvanized flue pipe with an outside diameter of seven inches will have a circumference in inches of MOST NEARLY equal to

   A. 22   B. 20   C. 19   D. 17

37. The sum of 2.6", 1.2", and 4.1" is

   A. 6.6"   B. 7.3"   C. 7.9"   D. 8.2"

38. An electric motor is NORMALLY rated in

   A. ohms   B. farads
   C. horsepower   D. megawatts

39. The one of the following electrical devices which USUALLY contains a magnetic coil is the

   A. battery   B. thermocouple
   C. relay   D. fustat

40. The MOST important requirement of a good boiler room report is that it should be   40.___
    A. prepared quickly
    B. short and clear
    C. very long and detailed
    D. shown to the building tenants

KEY (CORRECT ANSWERS)

1. D	11. D	21. A	31. C
2. B	12. A	22. B	32. B
3. C	13. A	23. A	33. A
4. D	14. B	24. B	34. C
5. A	15. A	25. C	35. A
6. B	16. B	26. A	36. A
7. A	17. D	27. B	37. C
8. C	18. C	28. D	38. C
9. C	19. D	29. A	39. C
10. D	20. A	30. D	40. B

EXAMINATION SECTION
TEST 1

DIRECTIONS: Each question or incomplete statement is followed by several suggested answers or completions. Select the one that BEST answers the question or completes the statement. *PRINT THE LETTER OF THE CORRECT ANSWER IN THE SPACE AT THE RIGHT.*

1. An instrument that is USUALLY mounted on a boiler control panel and which is read in inches of water is known as a(n) _____ gauge.

    A. pressure
    B. draft
    C. stack temperature
    D. Orsat indicator

    1.____

2. The type of pump which SHOULD be used to supply fuel oil to a low pressure boiler is the _____ pump.

    A. centrifugal
    B. diaphragm
    C. rotary gear
    D. reciprocating

    2.____

3. A thermostatic radiator trap which is working satisfactorily will

    A. *open* to pass the steam
    B. *open* to pass the condensate
    C. *close* to retain the cool air
    D. *close* to retain the condensate

    3.____

4. Readings of stack temperature and percentage of carbon dioxide are USEFUL in the boiler room in determining changes in the boiler's _____ efficiency.

    A. mechanical
    B. volumetric
    C. overall
    D. combustion

    4.____

5. In the start-up cycle of a boiler which is equipped with all of the following devices, the device that should be energized BEFORE all the others is the

    A. magnetic oil valve
    B. ignition transformer
    C. gas solenoid valve
    D. fresh air louvre motor

    5.____

6. The one of the following valves which is electrically operated is the _____ valve.

    A. pressure relief
    B. magnetic oil
    C. check
    D. thermostatic control

    6.____

7. In an installation where there is only one fuel oil pump set, a duplex strainer is PREFERABLY used because

    A. one side of the strainer can be cleaned without interrupting the flow of oil
    B. one side of the strainer will screen out much finer particles than the other side
    C. the flow of oil can be directed through both sides at the same time, thereby increasing the velocity of the oil
    D. cleaning of a duplex strainer is not required during the heating season

    7.____

8. A higher-than-normal vacuum reading on a gauge which is attached to the suction side of a fuel oil pump GENERALLY indicates that there is

    8.____

A. no oil in the tank
B. a clogged strainer in the suction line
C. a broken fitting in the suction line
D. worn packing on the pump

9. The one of the following which is NOT a possible point of entry of water leaking into the fuel oil storage tank is the

   A. fuel fill pipe can
   B. sounding well plug
   C. steam coil in a fuel oil heater
   D. fire box side of the furnace wall

10. When an air vaporstat which is connected to an automatic rotary cup oil burner senses the loss of primary air pressure in the fan housing, it DE-ENERGIZES the

    A. burner motor-starter coil
    B. magnetic oil valve
    C. secondary air damper control
    D. modutrol motor

11. A steam boiler which is externally fired and in which the hot gases pass through the tubes is COMMONLY known as a _____ boiler.

    A. scotch
    B. locomotive
    C. horizontal return tubular
    D. vertical tubular

12. The modulating pressuretrol on an automatic rotary cup oil-fired boiler controls the

    A. modutrol motor circuit
    B. magnetic oil valve
    C. burner motor starter
    D. electric heater

13. The reason for *blowing down* a boiler is to

    A. lower the boiler water level below the boiler tubes
    B. reduce the concentration of dissolved solids in the boiler water
    C. reduce the concentration of dissolved oxygen in the boiler water
    D. eliminate the need for treating the boiler water chemically

14. The one of the following boiler pressure-actuated devices which should be adjusted to operate at the HIGHEST pressure setting is the

    A. pop-safety valve
    B. manual-reset pressuretrol
    C. modulating pressuretrol
    D. limit pressuretrol

15. The BEST procedure for testing the operation of a low-water cutout is to lower the _____ until the burner shuts off.

    A. boiler water level rapidly
    B. boiler water level slowly
    C. water level in the water column rapidly
    D. water level in the water column slowly

16. If the water disappears from the gauge glass on a low-pressure oil-fired boiler, the FIRST action the boiler operator should take is to

    A. shut off the water
    B. add water to the boiler until the glass fills up to the correct level
    C. open the bottom blow-down valve
    D. blow down the water column

17. On a certain day, the lowest outside temperature was 20°F and the highest was 40°F. The number of degree days for this day is

    A. 25   B. 30   C. 35   D. 45

18. A vacuum return line pump should NOT be operated with the electrical control set for

    A. continuous operation
    B. float and vacuum control
    C. float control *only*
    D. vacuum control *only*

19. The PREFERRED location for a Dunham Selector is on the _____ exposure of the building.

    A. north   B. east   C. south   D. west

20. Maintaining a Dunham heat balancer in good working order requires annual cleaning of its

    A. radiator fins   B. relay contacts
    C. solenoid valve   D. fulcrum

21. An automatic device used for regulating air temperature is a(n)

    A. rheostat   B. aquastat   C. thermostat   D. duostat

22. Smoke alarms which must be installed on oil-fired boilers should create a loud signal and a red flashing light upon the emission of an air contaminant whose density, when compared to the standard smoke chart, appears DARKER than Number _____ on the chart.

    A. 1   B. 2   C. 3   D. 4

23. Samples for the testing of boiler water should be taken from the

    A. bottom blow-off   B. condensate tank
    C. water column   D. condensate return line

24. In a building which is heated by an oil-fired boiler, 2,100 gallons of fuel oil were burned in a period in which the degree days reached a total of 1,400.
    If all other conditions remained constant, the number of gallons of fuel oil that would be burned in this building during a period in which the degree days reached a total of 3,600 is

    A. 2,400   B. 2,900   C. 4,800   D. 5,400

25. Of the following fuels, the one with the HIGHEST viscosity is 25.____

    A. kerosene
    B. natural gas
    C. #6 oil
    D. #2 oil

KEY (CORRECT ANSWERS)

1. B
2. C
3. B
4. D
5. D

6. B
7. A
8. B
9. D
10. B

11. C
12. A
13. B
14. A
15. B

16. C
17. C
18. D
19. A
20. A

21. C
22. A
23. C
24. D
25. C

TEST 2

DIRECTIONS: Each question or incomplete statement is followed by several suggested answers or completions. Select the one that BEST answers the question or completes the statement. *PRINT THE LETTER OF THE CORRECT ANSWER IN THE SPACE AT THE RIGHT.*

1. An indicator card from a steam engine is MOST useful in

    A. determining the boiler pressure
    B. determining the engine speed
    C. adjusting the valve setting
    D. computing the mechanical efficiency

1.____

2. Which of the following statements is MOST NEARLY correct?

    A. A water tube boiler has the combustion gases inside the tubes.
    B. A scotch marine boiler has 2 drums.
    C. A brick set HRT boiler usually has a steel fire box.
    D. The circulation in a boiler may be either gravity or forced.

2.____

3. When the load on a mechanical stoker fired boiler plant furnishing steam for slide valve engine generators drops by 30%, the

    A. stoker should be shut down
    B. fan should be speeded up and the stoker slowed
    C. stoker should be speeded up and the air supply reduced
    D. stoker speed and air supply should be adjusted by reducing both

3.____

4. Which of the following statements is MOST NEARLY correct?

    A. All types of mechanical stokers may be used with equal efficiency under all types of boilers.
    B. Most stokers are designed with a weak member.
    C. The best type of stoker to use is not dependent upon the type of fuel available.
    D. The advisability of installing stokers is not dependent upon the load.

4.____

5. The number and size of safety valves required on a high pressure boiler is dependent upon the

    A. size of the boiler drums
    B. amount of heating surface
    C. number of pounds of fuel burned per square foot of grate per hour
    D. size of the steam main

5.____

6. In changing over a boiler from high pressure (150 lbs. per square inch) to 10 lbs. per square inch, it is usually NECESSARY to

    A. *increase* the size of the safety valves
    B. *decrease* the grate area
    C. *increase* the size of the feed water piping
    D. *increase* the size of the blow down piping

6.____

7. A boiler feed injector becomes temporarily steam bound. To correct this condition, the MOST proper action to take is to

   A. increase boiler pressure
   B. reduce suction lift
   C. wrap it with cold rags
   D. bank fire

8. The PROPER method of laying up a steam boiler for a period of less than one month is to

   A. drain all the water and let the boiler dry out
   B. fill it with treated water to the top of the tubes
   C. fill it with treated water to the stop valve
   D. fill it with treated water to the level of the upper try cock

9. In the winter time, heating complaints by tenants should be investigated

   A. only if there are several complaints from one building
   B. only if the outside temperature is below 40°F
   C. immediately
   D. by the assistant superintendent

10. Compared to the input of the electric ignition transformer associated with #6 oil burners, the output is _____ voltage, _____ current.

    A. higher; higher
    B. higher; lower
    C. lower; higher
    D. lower; lower

11. A pressure regulator valve in a compressed air line should be

    A. preceded by a water and oil separator
    B. preceded by a solenoid valve
    C. followed by a water and oil separator
    D. followed by a solenoid valve

12. A preventive maintenance program in a boiler room should provide for the routine periodic replacement of

    A. badly leaking boiler tubes
    B. electric motors
    C. safety valve springs
    D. programmer electronic tubes

13. Steam heated hot water tank coils can be tested for leaks by

    A. chemically testing the domestic hot water leaving the tank
    B. chemically testing the condensate leaving the coil
    C. pressure testing the domestic water in the tank
    D. pressure testing the condensate return

14. The chemical which is added to boiler water to reduce its oxygen content is sodium

    A. carbonate   B. chloride   C. alginate   D. sulphite

15. Wear in the sleeve bearings of an electric motor is MOST likely to result in a change in the

    A. pole spacing
    B. armature balance
    C. air gap
    D. line frequency

16. Assume that only the first few coils of a hot water convector used for heating a room are hot.
    To correct this, you should FIRST

    A. increase the water pressure
    B. increase the water temperature
    C. bleed the air out of the convector
    D. clean the convector pipes

17. When priming occurs in a boiler,

    A. the fire will be extinguished
    B. the steam becomes superheated and too dry
    C. the fire tubes become overheated and may crack
    D. water particles are carried over with the steam into the steam lines

18. One of the ways to prevent or reduce the amount of smoke from a furnace is to

    A. reduce the quantity of air supplied to the fire box
    B. supply coal in large quantities and no more than twice a day
    C. cool the fire bed to prevent high temperatures in the fire box
    D. keep live coals at the top of the fire bed

19. Of the following, the SMALLEST size coal is

    A. chestnut   B. egg   C. buckwheat   D. pea

20. If coal is to be stored, the following precaution should be followed:

    A. Coal should be piled in conical piles rather than horizontal layers
    B. Coal should be placed in storage on hot summer days
    C. Avoid alternate wetting and drying of coal
    D. Coal should be piled no more than three feet deep

21. The HRT boiler contains

    A. fire tubes in which hot gases flow
    B. water tubes in which water flows to form steam
    C. no horizontal return tubes
    D. no way in which a vacuum return can be connected

22. A room is properly heated in the winter time when the temperature is about _____ °F and the relative humidity is _____ %.

    A. 70; 40 to 60
    B. 78; 40 to 60
    C. 65; 30
    D. 75; 90

23. The average temperature on a day in January is 30°F. This would be called a _____ degree day.

    A. 40   B. 35   C. 30   D. 25

24. The term BTU is used in connection with

    A. heating quality of a fuel
    B. the size of boiler tubes
    C. radiator fittings
    D. heating qualities of radiators

25. Which one of the following is NOT the cause of clinker formation?

    A. Poor quality coal
    B. Thick fires
    C. Closed ashpit doors
    D. Water sprayed into the ashpit at intervals during the day

KEY (CORRECT ANSWERS)

1.	C	11.	A
2.	D	12.	D
3.	D	13.	B
4.	B	14.	D
5.	B	15.	C
6.	A	16.	C
7.	C	17.	D
8.	C	18.	D
9.	C	19.	C
10.	B	20.	C

21. A
22. A
23. B
24. A
25. D

TEST 3

DIRECTIONS: Each question or incomplete statement is followed by several suggested answers or completions. Select the one that BEST answers the question or completes the statement. *PRINT THE LETTER OF THE CORRECT ANSWER IN THE SPACE AT THE RIGHT.*

1. With steam at a temperature of 365°F in a boiler, which of the following stack gas temperatures would you consider to be good usual operating practice in a plant without economizers, air preheaters, and the like?

    A. 300°F   B. 500°F   C. 700°F   D. 900°F

    1.____

2. The percentage of CO_2 in the stack gases is an indication of the

    A. rate of combustion in the furnace
    B. rate at which excess air is supplied to the furnace
    C. rate of carbon monoxide production in the furnace
    D. temperature of combustion

    2.____

3. In the most usual type of large capacity oil burner using #6 oil, under *fully automatic* control, the atomization of the oil is produced MAINLY by the

    A. pressure from the pump
    B. pressure from the secondary air fan
    C. oil temperature from the heater
    D. rotation of the burner assembly by the motor

    3.____

4. Of the following, the figure which comes the CLOSEST to indicating the number of degree days in a normal heating season in New York City is

    A. 3000   B. 4000   C. 5000   D. 6000

    4.____

5. In which of the following methods of steam generation would you expect to obtain reasonably continuous values of CO_2 CLOSEST to the perfect CO_2 value?
Automatic

    A. stoker firing with temperature recorder
    B. stoker firing with *hold five timer*
    C. oil firing with *stack switch*
    D. oil firing with *haze regulator*

    5.____

6. The loss of heat in stack gases for heavy fuel oil is
HIGHEST when the CO_2 content is _____% and the stack temperature is _____°

    A. 12; 500   B. 8; 600   C. 6; 700   D. 14; 600

    6.____

7. A badly sooted HRT boiler under coal firing will show a _____ than a clean boiler.

    A. higher CO_2 value
    B. lower CO_2 value
    C. higher stack temperature
    D. lower draft loss

    7.____

8. A unit heater condensing 50 lbs. of low pressure steam per hour would be rated MOST NEARLY at _____ square feet E.D.R.

   A. 50 B. 100 C. 150 D. 200

9. One horsepower MOST NEARLY equals

   A. 550 ft.-lbs. per second
   B. 3300 ft.-lbs. per minute
   C. 55000 ft.-lbs. per hour
   D. 10000 ft.-lbs. per minute

10. A pressure gauge attached to a standpipe system shows a pressure of 36 pounds per square inch.
    The head of water, in feet, above the gauge is MOST NEARLY

    A. 24 B. 36 C. 60 D. 83

11. Of the following, the term *vapor barrier* would MOST likely be associated with

    A. electric service installation
    B. insulation materials
    C. fuel oil tank installation
    D. domestic gas piping

12. Pitot tubes are used to

    A. test feed water for impurities
    B. measure air or gas flow in a duct
    C. prevent overheating of elements of a steam gauge
    D. control the ignition system of an oil burner

13. In warm air heating and in ventilating systems, laboratories and kitchens should NOT be equipped with return ducts in order to

    A. keep air velocities in other returns as high as possible
    B. reduce fire hazards
    C. reduce the possibility of circulating odors through the system
    D. keep the temperature high in these rooms

14. One square foot of equivalent direct steam radiation (EDR) is equivalent to a heat emission of _____ BTU per _____.

    A. 150; hour
    B. 240; minute
    C. 150; minute
    D. 240; hour

15. Of the following, the one which is LEAST likely to cause continuous vibration of an operating motor is

    A. a faulty starting circuit
    B. excessive belt tension
    C. the misalignment of motor and driven equipment
    D. loose bearings

16. The function of a steam trap is to

    A. remove sediment and dirt from steam
    B. remove air and non-condensible gases from steam
    C. relieve excessive steam pressure to the atmosphere
    D. remove condensate from a pipe or an apparatus

17. The temperature at which air is just saturated with the moisture present in it is called its

    A. relative humidity
    B. absolute humidity
    C. humid temperature
    D. dew point

18. Of the following, the one which is NOT a general class of oil burners is the _____ atomizing.

    A. water
    B. rotary cup
    C. mechanical
    D. air

19. Of the following, the one which should be between a boiler and its safety valve is

    A. a swing check valve of a size larger than that of the safety valve
    B. a butterfly valve located in the boiler nozzle
    C. a gate valve of the same nominal size as that of the safety valve
    D. no valve of any type

20. The term *spinner cup* refers to

    A. screw-type stokers
    B. gun-type oil burners
    C. rotary-type oil burners
    D. chain grate stokers

21. A gun-type burner is often used on a

    A. pot-type oil burner
    B. low pressure gas boiler
    C. coal underfeed stoker boiler
    D. high pressure oil-fired boiler

22. Of the following, the action that should be taken as the FIRST step if a properly adjusted safety valve on a steam boiler *pops off* when in operation is

    A. open the draft
    B. add more water to the boiler
    C. wire the valve shut
    D. reduce the draft

23. When the water gets below the safe level in an operating boiler, it is BEST to

    A. add new water up to the safe level and open up the fire so that the water will heat quickly
    B. check the fire and let the boiler cool down before new water is added
    C. add new water to the boiler immediately
    D. check the fire and empty the boiler

24. Vents on fuel oil storage tanks are used to
    A. fill the fuel tanks
    B. allow air to escape during filling
    C. check oil flash points
    D. make tank fuel soundings

25. Of the following, the MOST desirable way to remove carbon deposits from the atomizing cup of an oil burner is to
    A. apply a hot flame to the carbonized surfaces to burn off the carbon deposits
    B. use kerosene to loosen the deposits and wipe with a soft cloth
    C. wash the cup with a mild trisodium phosphate solution and dry with a cloth
    D. use a scraper, followed by light rubbing with emery cloth

KEY (CORRECT ANSWERS)

1.	B	11.	B
2.	B	12.	B
3.	D	13.	C
4.	C	14.	D
5.	D	15.	A
6.	C	16.	D
7.	C	17.	D
8.	D	18.	A
9.	A	19.	D
10.	D	20.	C

21. D
22. D
23. B
24. B
25. B

ARITHMETICAL REASONING
EXAMINATION SECTION
TEST 1

DIRECTIONS: Each question or incomplete statement is followed by several suggested answers or completions. Select the one that BEST answers the question or completes the statement. PRINT THE LETTER OF THE CORRECT ANSWER IN THE SPACE AT THE RIGHT.

1. A custodial assistant takes an average of forty minutes to mop 1,000 square feet of floor. The amount of time this custodial assistant should take to mop the floor of a rectangular corridor eight feet wide by sixty feet long is, on the average, MOST NEARLY _____ minutes.

   A. 10   B. 20   C. 30   D. 40

   1.____

2. An auditorium eighty feet by 100 feet must be swept in one hour.
   If each custodial assistant takes fifteen minutes to sweep 1,000 square feet of auditorium area, the number of custodial assistants that must be assigned to complete the sweeping in one hour is

   A. 1   B. 2   C. 3   D. 4

   2.____

3. A detergent manufacturer recommends mixing 8 ounces of detergent in one gallon of water to prepare a cleaning solution.
   The amount of the same detergent which should be mixed with thirty gallons of water to obtain the same strength cleaning solution is _____ ounces.

   A. 24   B. 30   C. 240   D. 380

   3.____

4. The floor area of a corridor 8 feet wide and 72 feet long is MOST NEARLY _____ square feet.

   A. 80   B. 420   C. 580   D. 870

   4.____

5. A water tank that is 5 feet in diameter and 30 feet high has a volume of MOST NEARLY _____ cubic feet.

   A. 150   B. 250   C. 600   D. 1,200

   5.____

6. The circumference of a circle with a radius of 5 inches is MOST NEARLY _____ inches.

   A. 31.3   B. 30.0   C. 20.1   D. 13.4

   6.____

7. Suppose that you are the custodian-engineer and an employee works for you at the rate of $8.70 per hour with time and one-half paid for time worked after 40 hours in one week. His gross pay for working 53 hours in one week is MOST NEARLY

   A. $461.10   B. $482.10   C. $487.65   D. $517.65

   7.____

69

8. Suppose that you are the custodian-engineer and one of your employees has gotten gross earnings of $437.10 for the week, all of which is subject to deductions at the rate of 4.8%.
   The amount which should be deducted from the employee's gross earnings for the week is MOST NEARLY

   A. $2.10 B. $14.70 C. $17.70 D. $20.97

9. The directions on the label of a bottle of detergent call for mixing four ounces of detergent with one gallon of water to make a cleaning solution for washing floors. In order to obtain a larger amount of solution of the same strength, one quart of the detergent should be mixed with _____ gallons of water.

   A. 2 B. 4 C. 6 D. 8

10. The area of a lawn which is 58 feet wide by 96 feet long is MOST NEARLY _____ square feet.

    A. 5,000 B. 5,500 C. 6,000 D. 6,500

11. In a building which is heated by an oil-fired boiler, 2,100 gallons of fuel oil were burned in a period in which the degree days reached a total of 1,400.
    If all other conditions remained constant, the number of gallons of fuel oil that would be burned in this building during a period in which the degree days reached a total of 3,600 is

    A. 2,400 B. 2,900 C. 4,800 D. 5,400

12. The instructions for mixing a powdered cleaner in water state, *Mix three ounces of powder in a 14-quart pail three-quarters full of water.* A cleaner asks you how much powdered cleaner he should use in a mop truck containing 28 gallons of water to obtain the same strength solution.
    The CORRECT answer is _____ ounces of powder.

    A. 6 B. 8 C. 24 D. 32

13. A custodian-engineer wishes to order sponges in the most economical manner. Keeping in mind that large sponges can be cut up into many smaller sizes, the one of the following that has the LEAST cost per cubic inch of sponge is

    A. 2" x 4" x 6" sponges @ $.48
    B. 4" x 8" x 12" sponges @ $2.88
    C. 4" x 6" x 36" sponges @ $9.60
    D. 6" x 8" x 32" sponges @ $19.20

14. Two cleaners swept four corridors in 24 minutes. Each corridor measured 12 feet x 176 feet.
    The space swept per man per minute was MOST NEARLY _____ square feet.

    A. 50 B. 90 C. 180 D. 350

15. Kerosene costs 60 cents a quart.
    At that rate, two gallons would cost

    A. $2.40 B. $3.60 C. $4.80 D. $6.00

16. The instructions on a container of cleaning compound states, *Mix one pound of compound in 5 gallons of water.* Using these instructions, the amount of compound which should be added to 15 quarts of water is MOST likely _____ ounces.

    A. 3   B. 8   C. 12   D. 48

17. Suppose that you are the custodian-engineer and one of your employees has gross earnings of $582.80 for the week, all of which is subject to Social Security deductions at the rate of 4.8%.
    The amount which should be deducted from the employee's gross earnings for the week is MOST NEARLY

    A. $2.80   B. $19.60   C. $23.60   D. $27.96

18. Suppose that you are a custodian-engineer and an employee works for you at the rate of $11.60 per hour with time and one-half paid for time worked after 40 hours in one week. His gross pay for working 53 hours in one week is MOST NEARLY

    A. $614.80   B. $642.80   C. $650.20   D. $690.20

19. The volume, in cubic feet, of a cylindrical tank 6 feet in diameter x 35 feet long is MOST NEARLY

    A. 210   B. 990   C. 1,260   D. 3,960

20. A room 12 feet wide by 25 feet long has a floor area of _____ square feet.

    A. 37   B. 200   C. 300   D. 400

21. How many hours will it take a worker to sweep a floor space of 2,800 square feet if he sweeps at the rate of 800 square feet per hour?

    A. 8   B. 6 1/2   C. 3 1/2   D. 2 1/2

22. One gallon of water contains

    A. 2 quarts   B. 4 quarts   C. 2 pints   D. 4 pints

23. A standard cleaning solution is prepared by mixing 4 ounces of detergent powder in 2 gallons of water.
    The number of ounces of detergent powder needed for the same strength solution in 5 gallons of water is

    A. 4   B. 6   C. 8   D. 10

24. The ceiling of a room which measures 20 feet x 30 feet is to be given two coats of paint. If one gallon of paint will cover 500 square feet, the two coats of paint will require a MINIMUM of _____ gallons.

    A. 1.5   B. 2   C. 2.4   D. 3.2

25. The floor area of a room which measures 10 feet long by 10 feet wide is _____ square feet.

    A. 20   B. 40   C. 100   D. 1,000

KEY (CORRECT ANSWERS)

1.	B	11.	D
2.	B	12.	D
3.	C	13.	B
4.	C	14.	C
5.	C	15.	C
6.	A	16.	C
7.	D	17.	D
8.	D	18.	D
9.	D	19.	B
10.	B	20.	C

21. C
22. B
23. D
24. C
25. C

SOLUTIONS TO PROBLEMS

1. (8')(60') = 480 sq.ft. Let x = required time in minutes.

   Then, $\dfrac{40}{1000} = \dfrac{x}{480}$. Solving, x = 19.2 or nearly 20.

2. (80')(100') = 8000 sq.ft. Each custodian can sweep (1000)(4) = 4000 sq.ft. in 1 hour. Then, 8000 ÷ 4000 = 2.

3. (8)(30) = 240 ounces

4. (8')(72') = 576 sq.ft. or nearly 580 sq.ft.

5. Volume = $(\pi)(2.5')^2(30') \approx$ 589 cu.ft. or nearly 600 cu.ft.

6. Circumference = $(2\pi)(5") \approx$ 31.3 sq.in.

7. ($8.70)(40) + ($13.05)(13) = $517.65

8. ($437.10)(.048) ≈ $20.97

9. 1 quart = 32 oz. Then, 32 ÷ 4 = 8 gallons of water

10. (58')(96') = 5568 sq.ft., which is closest to 5500 sq.ft.

11. Let x = number of gallons. Then, $\dfrac{2100}{1400} = \dfrac{x}{3600}$. Solving, x = 5400

12. (.75)(14)(.25) = 2.625 gallons of water. Let x = number of ounces of powder needed. Then, $\dfrac{3}{2.625} = \dfrac{x}{28}$. Solving, x = 32

13. For selection B, (4")(8")(12") = 384 cu.in., and the cost per cubic inch = $2.88 ÷ 384 = $.0075. This is lower than selections A ($.01), C ($.011), or D ($.015).

14. Two men sweep (4)(12')(176') = 8448 total sq.ft. in 24 min. = 352 sq.ft. per min. Each man sweeps 176 sq.ft. per min ≈ 180 sq.ft. per min.

15. Two gallons = 8 quarts. Then, ($.60)(8) = $4.80

16. 15 quarts = 3.75 gallons of water. Let x = required number of ounces of compound. Then, $\dfrac{16}{5} = \dfrac{x}{3.75}$. Solving, x = 12

17. ($582.80)(.048) ≈ $27.96

18. ($11.60 × 40) + ($17.40)(13) = $690.20

19. Volume = $(\pi)(3')^2(35') \approx$ 990 cu.ft.

20. (12')(25') = 300 sq.ft.

21. 2800 ÷ 800 = 3 1/2 hours

22. One gallon = 4 quarts

23. Let x = required number of ounces. Then, $\frac{4}{2} = \frac{x}{5}$. Solving, x = 10

24. 2 coats means (2)(20')(30') = 1200 sq.ft. Then, 1200 ÷ 500 = 2.4 gallons

25. (10')(10') = 100 sq.ft.

TEST 2

DIRECTIONS: Each question or incomplete statement is followed by several suggested answers or completions. Select the one that BEST answers the question or completes the statement. *PRINT THE LETTER OF THE CORRECT ANSWER IN THE SPACE AT THE RIGHT.*

1. Assume that a certain elevator starter is at work 8 hours a day, which includes 1 hour for lunch and two 15-minute relief periods. The rest of the workday the starter is performing his duties.
   If the starter works 4 days, the TOTAL amount of time the starter will actually be performing his duties is _____ hours.

   A. 24   B. 26   C. 28   D. 32

2. Assume that a certain bank of 18 elevators operating at full capacity could move 3,240 passengers an hour from the main lobby.
   The number of passengers that one of these elevators could move from the lobby every 15 minutes is, on the average,

   A. 12   B. 22   C. 45   D. 180

3. In a certain agency, the amount of absence due to injury or illness was an average of 6 hours a month for each employee.
   If this agency had 335 employees, the TOTAL number of hours lost in a year due to injury or sickness was

   A. 4,020   B. 20,100   C. 24,120   D. 28,140

4. Assume that in a certain building the elevators must handle 16% of the building population during a peak traffic period.
   If the building population is 2,825, the TOTAL number of people the elevators must handle during a peak traffic period is

   A. 396   B. 424   C. 436   D. 452

5. From his coin bank, a boy took 3 half dollars, 8 quarters, 7 dimes, 6 nickels, and 9 pennies to deposit in his school savings account.
   Express in dollars and cents the TOTAL amount of money he deposited.

   A. $2.82   B. $4.59   C. $6.42   D. $7.52

6. If a roast that requires 1 hour and 40 minutes of roasting time has been in the oven for 55 minutes, how many more minutes of roasting time are required?

   A. 30   B. 36   C. 45   D. 55

7. On the first day of its drive, a school raised $40, which was 33 1/3% of its Red Cross quota.
   How much was the quota?

   A. $120   B. $130   C. $140   D. $150

8. When 0.750 is divided by 0.875, the answer is MOST NEARLY

   A. 0.250   B. 0.312   C. 0.624   D. 0.857

75

9. The circumference of a 6-inch diameter circle is MOST NEARLY _____ feet.

   A. 1.57　　　B. 2.1　　　C. 2.31　　　D. 4.24

10. An 18" piece of cable that weighs 3 pounds per foot has a total weight of _____ pounds.

    A. 5.5　　　B. 4.5　　　C. 3.0　　　D. 1.5

11. The sum of 0.135, 0.040, 0.812, and 0.961 is

    A. 1.424　　　B. 1.625　　　C. 1.843　　　D. 1.948

12. If an elevator carries a load of 1,600 pounds uniformly distributed on a 4 feet by 5 feet floor, the weight per square foot is _____ pounds.

    A. 98　　　B. 80　　　C. 65　　　D. 40

13. If one cubic inch of lead weighs one-quarter of a pound, the weight of a bar of lead 1" high by 2" wide by 8" long is _____ pounds.

    A. 1.8　　　B. 2.5　　　C. 3.1　　　D. 4

14. Assume that 8 mechanics have been assigned to do a job that must be finished in 5 days. At the end of 3 days, the men have completed only half the job.
    In order to complete the job on time in the remaining 2 days, the MINIMUM number of extra men that should be assigned is

    A. 2　　　B. 3　　　C. 4　　　D. 6

15. An elevator supply manufacturer quotes a list price of $625 less 10 and 5 percent for ten contactors.
    The actual cost for these ten contactors is MOST NEARLY

    A. $562　　　B. $554　　　C. $534　　　D. $522

16. To find the largest number of passengers, including the operator, allowed to ride in an elevator, divide the rated capacity of the elevator by 150.
    According to this rule, what is the LARGEST number of passengers NOT counting the operator that may be carried in an elevator with a rated capacity of 3,000 lbs.?

    A. 18　　　B. 19　　　C. 20　　　D. 21

17. Suppose that the work schedule for operators is 5 days a week, 8 hours a day.
    In a period of 4 weeks, with no holidays, how many hours will you be required to be on duty?

    A. 160　　　B. 180　　　C. 200　　　D. 225

18. Mr. Jones takes $200 to cover his expenses for a week. He spends $6.00 for carfare coming to work and $6.00 for carfare going home. He buys a $1 newspaper each day and spends $16.00 for lunch and $5.00 for cigarettes each day.
    How much money does he have left at the end of a 5-day work week?

    A. $30.00　　　B. $55.00　　　C. $100.00　　　D. $170.00

19. Twelve hundred employees work in an office building. 19.____
Twenty percent of these employees work on the 4th floor and 25% work on the 5th floor.
The TOTAL number of employees who work on the 4th and 5th floors together is

    A. 240   B. 300   C. 540   D. 660

20. An elevator makes one roundtrip every 5 minutes, on the average. 20.____
How many roundtrips does it make between 8:15 A.M. and 9:45 A.M.?

    A. 12   B. 18   C. 20   D. 22

21. The floor of an elevator car measures 7 feet by 8 feet 6 inches. 21.____
How many square feet of linoleum would be needed to cover this floor?

    A. 31   B. 42   C. 59 1/2   D. 62 1/2

Questions 22-25.

   DIRECTIONS: Each question consists of a statement. You are to indicate whether the statement is TRUE (T) or FALSE (F).

22. In a city building, there are 20 elevators. If on one day five percent of the elevators are out of order, the number of elevators out of order is 2. 22.____

23. An elevator operator puts in 32 hours of overtime in January, 26 hours in February, 10 hours in March, 10 hours in April, and 27 hours in May. The average amount of overtime this operator worked per month for these five months is 21 hours. 23.____

24. A large city building normally has 45 elevator operators on its day shift. The vacation rules require that only 1/5 be allowed away at any time. The number of operators that may be on vacation at one time is nine. 24.____

25. In a six-story city building, there are 13 offices on the first floor, 19 offices on the second floor, 18 offices on the third floor, 17 offices on the fourth floor, 21 offices on the fifth floor, and 23 offices on the sixth floor. The total number of offices in this building is 109. 25.____

KEY (CORRECT ANSWERS)

1.	B	11.	D
2.	C	12.	B
3.	C	13.	D
4.	D	14.	C
5.	B	15.	C
6.	C	16.	B
7.	A	17.	A
8.	D	18.	A
9.	A	19.	C
10.	B	20.	B

21. C
22. F
23. T
24. T
25. F

SOLUTIONS TO PROBLEMS

1. 4(8-1-.5) = 26 hours

2. Each elevator can move 3240 ÷ 18 = 180 passengers per hour, which = 45 passengers per 15 minutes.

3. (335)(6)(12) = 24,120 hours per year.

4. (2825)(.16) = 452

5. (3)(.50) + (8)(.25) + (7)(.10) + (6)(.05) + (9)(.01) = $4.59

6. 1 hr. 40 min. - 55 min. = 100 min. - 55 min. = 45 min.

7. $40 ÷ $33\frac{1}{3}$% = $40 ÷ $\frac{1}{3}$ = $120

8. .750 ÷ .875 ≈ .857

9. Circumference = ($\frac{1}{2}$')(π) ≈ 1.57'

10. 18" ÷ 12" = 1.5. Then, (1.5)(3) = 4.5 lbs.

11. .135 + .040 + .812 + .961 = 1.948

12. (4')(5') = 20 sq.ft. Then, 1600 ÷ 20 = 80 lbs. per sq.ft.

13. (1")(2")(8") = 16 cu.in. Then, (16)(1/4) = 4 pounds

14. 8 men x 3 cars = 50% of work; 24 man-days = 50% of work; 48 man-days = 100%; 24 man-days ÷ 2 days = 12 men per day = 4 extra men

15. ($625)(.90)(.95) ≈ $534

16. 3000 ÷ 150 = 20 people, including the operator. Thus, only 19 passengers are allowed.

17. (8)(5)(4) = 160 hours

18. $200 - 5($6.00+$6.00+$1+$16.00+$5.00) = $30.00

19. (1200)(20%+25%) = (1200)(.45) = 540

20. 9:45 AM - 8:15 AM = 90 min. Then, 90 ÷ 5 = 18 roundtrips

21. (7')(8 1/2') = 59 1/2 sq.ft.

22. False; (20)(.05) = 1, not 2.

23. True. (32+26+10+10+27) ÷ 5 = 21

24. True. (45)(1/5) = 9

25. False. 13 + 19 + 18 + 17 + 21 + 23 = 111, not 109

TEST 3

DIRECTIONS: Each question or incomplete statement is followed by several suggested answers or completions. Select the one that BEST answers the question or completes the statement. *PRINT THE LETTER OF THE CORRECT ANSWER IN THE SPACE AT THE RIGHT.*

1. When 60,987 is added to 27,835, the answer is
   A. 80,712 B. 80,822 C. 87,712 D. 88,822

2. The sum of 693 + 787 + 946 + 355 + 731 is
   A. 3,512 B. 3,502 C. 3,412 D. 3,402

3. When 2,586 is subtracted from 3,003, the answer is
   A. 417 B. 527 C. 1,417 D. 1,527

4. When 1.32 is subtracted from 52.6, the answer is
   A. 3.94 B. 5.128 C. 39.4 D. 51.28

5. When 56 is multiplied by 438, the answer is
   A. 840 B. 4,818 C. 24,528 D. 48,180

6. When 8.7 is multiplied by .34, the answer is MOST NEARLY
   A. 2.9 B. 3.0 C. 29.5 D. 29.6

7. When 1/2 is divided by 2/3, the answer is
   A. 1/3 B. 3/4 C. 1 1/3 D. 3

8. When 8,340 is divided by 38, the answer is MOST NEARLY
   A. 210 B. 218 C. 219 D. 220

9. Assume that a helper earns $11.16 an hour and that he works 250 seven-hour days a year.
   His gross yearly salary will be
   A. $19,430 B. $19,530 C. $19,650 D. $19,780

10. On a certain map, a distance of 10 miles is represented by 1/2 inch.
    If two towns are 3 1/2 inches apart on this map, express, in miles, the actual distance between the two towns.
    A. 70 B. 80 C. 90 D. 100

11. The area of the triangle shown at the right is _____ square inches.
    A. 120
    B. 240
    C. 360
    D. 480

12. The sum of 1/3 + 2/5 + 5/6 is 12._____

    A. 1 17/30   B. 1 3/5   C. 1 5/8   D. 1 5/6

13. The sum of the following dimensions, 3'2 1/4", 0'8 7/8", 2'6 3/8", 2'9 3/4", and 1'0", is 13._____

    A. 9'2 7/8"   B. 10'3 1/4"
    C. 10'7 3/7"   D. 11'4 1/4"

14. If the scale of a drawing is 1/8" to the foot, then a 1/2" measurement on the drawing would represent an actual length of _____ feet. 14._____

    A. 2   B. 4   C. 8   D. 16

15. Assume that an area measures 78 feet by 96 feet.
    The number of square feet in this area is 15._____

    A. 7,478   B. 7,488   C. 7,498   D. 7,508

16. If a can of paint costs $17.50, four dozen cans of this paint will cost 16._____

    A. $837.50   B. $840.00   C. $842.50   D. $845.00

17. The number of square feet in 1 square yard is 17._____

    A. 3   B. 6   C. 9   D. 12

18. The sum of 4 1/2 inches, 3 1/4 inches, and 7 1/2 inches is 1 foot _____ inches. 18._____

    A. 3   B. 3 1/4   C. 3 1/2   D. 4

19. If a room is 10 feet by 18 feet, the number of square feet of floor space in it is 19._____

    A. 1,800   B. 180   C. 90   D. 28

20. A jacket that was marked at $12.50 was sold for $10.
    What was the rate of discount on the marked price? 20._____

    A. 10%   B. 15%   C. 18%   D. 20%

Questions 21-25.

DIRECTIONS: Each question consists of a statement. You are to indicate whether the statement is TRUE (T) or FALSE (F).

21. Three-eighths (3/8") of an inch is equivalent to .0375". 21._____

22. A floor measuring 12 feet by 9 feet contains 36 sq.ft. 22._____

23. A box measuring 18 inches square and 16 inches deep will have a volume of 36 cubic feet. 23._____

24. If the charge for a long distance telephone call is 50¢ for the first 5 minutes and 7? for each minute after that, then for 85¢ a person could speak for 10 minutes. 24._____

25. If 15 gallons of gasoline cost $14.85 and you use up 10 gallons, then the value of the gasoline which is still left is $4.95. 25._____

KEY (CORRECT ANSWERS)

1.	D	11.	A
2.	A	12.	A
3.	A	13.	B
4.	D	14.	B
5.	C	15.	B
6.	B	16.	B
7.	B	17.	C
8.	C	18.	B
9.	B	19.	B
10.	A	20.	D

21. F
22. F
23. F
24. T
25. T

SOLUTIONS TO PROBLEMS

1. $60{,}987 + 27{,}835 = 88{,}822$

2. $693 + 787 + 946 + 355 + 731 = 3512$

3. $3003 - 2586 = 417$

4. $52.6 - 1.32 = 51.28$

5. $(56)(438) = 24{,}528$

6. $(8.7)(.34) = 2.958 \approx 3.0$

7. $\dfrac{1}{2} \div \dfrac{2}{3} = \dfrac{1}{2} \cdot \dfrac{3}{2} = \dfrac{3}{4}$

8. $8340 \div 38 \approx 219.47 \approx 219$

9. $(\$11.16)(7)(250) = \$19{,}530$

10. $3\ 1/2" \div 1/2" = 7$. Then, $(7)(10) = 70$ miles

11. Area $= (1/2)(10")(24") = 120$ sq.in.

12. $\dfrac{1}{3} + \dfrac{2}{5} + \dfrac{5}{6} = \dfrac{10}{30} + \dfrac{12}{30} + \dfrac{25}{30} = \dfrac{47}{30} = 1\dfrac{17}{30}$

13. $3'2\ 1/4" + 0'8\ 7/8" + 2'6\ 3/8" + 2'9\ 3/4" + 1'0" = 8'25\ 18/8" = 10'3\ 1/4"$

14. $1/2" \div 1/8" = 4$. Then, $(4)(1\text{ ft.}) = 4$ ft.

15. $(78')(96') = 7488$ sq.ft.

16. $(48)(\$17.50) = \$840.00$

17. 1 sq.yd. $= (3)(3) = 9$ sq.ft.

18. $4\ 1/2" + 3\ 1/4" + 7\ 1/2" = 14\ 5/4" = 1$ foot $3\ 1/4$ inches

19. $(10')(18') = 180$ sq.ft.

20. $\$12.50 - \$10 = \$2.50$. Then, $\$2.50 \div \$12.50 = .20 = 20\%$

21. False. $3/8" = .375"$, not $.0375"$

22. False. $(12')(9') = 108$ sq.ft., not 36 sq.ft.

23. False. $(18")(18")(16") = 5184$ cu.in. $= 3$ cu.ft., not 36 cu.ft.
    Note: 1 cu.ft. = 1728 cu.in.

24. True. The cost for 10 minutes $= .50 + (.07)(10-5) = .85$

25. True. $\$14.85 \div 15 = \$.99$ per gallon. The value of 5 gallons $= (5)(\$.99) = \$4.95$

BASIC FUNDAMENTALS OF BOILERS

TABLE OF CONTENTS

		Page
I.	NATURE	1
II.	CLASSIFICATION	2
	A. Location of Fire and Water Spaces	2
	B. Size of Tubes	2
	C. Type of Circulation	2
	D. Type of Superheat	3
III.	TERMINOLOGY	3
	A. Fire Room and Boiler Room	4
	B. Boiler Emergency Station	4
	C. Boiler Full-Power Capacity	4
	D. Boiler Overload Capacity	4
	E. Superheater Outlet Pressure	4
	F. Steam Drum Pressure	4
	G. Design Pressure	4
	H. Operating Pressure	4
	I. Boiler Efficiency	4
	J. Fire Room Efficiency	4
	K. Total Heating Surface	5
	L. Generating Surface	5
	M. Superheater Surface	5
	N. Economizer Surface	5
	O. Steaming Hours	5

BASIC FUNDAMENTALS OF BOILERS

I. NATURE

The boiler is the source or high-temperature region of the thermos-dynamic cycle. The steam that is generated in the boiler is led to the turbines, where its thermal energy is converted into mechanical energy (work) which drives the unit and provides power for vital services.

In essence, a boiler is merely a container in which water can be boiled and steam generated. A tea kettle on a stove is basically a boiler, although a rather inefficient one. Note that the steam is generated in one vessel and superheated in another, since it is impossible to raise the temperature of the steam above the temperature of the boiling water as long as the two are in contact with each other.

In designing a boiler which must produce a large amount of steam, it is obviously necessary to find some means of providing a larger amount of heat-transfer surface than could be provided by a vessel shaped like a tea kettle. In most modern boilers, the steam generating surface consists of hundreds and hundreds of tubes, which provide a maximum amount of heat-transfer surface in a relatively small space. As a rule, the tubes communicate with a steam drum at the top of a boiler and with water drums and headers at the bottom of the boiler. The tubes and part of the drums are enclosed in an insulated capsule which has space inside it for the furnace. A boiler appears to be a fairly complicated piece of equipment when it is considered with all its fittings, piping, and accessories; it may be helpful, therefore, to remember that the basic components of a saturated-steam boiler are merely the tubes, the drums, and headers, and the furnace.

Practically all boilers used in propulsion are designed to produce both saturated steam and superheated steam. To our basic boiler, therefore, we must now add another component: the superheater. The superheater on most boilers consist of headers, usually located at the back of the boiler, and a number of superheater tubes which communicate with the headers. Saturated steam from the steam drum is led through the superheater; since the steam is now no longer in contact with the water from which it was generated, the steam becomes superheated as additional heat is supplied. In some boilers, there is a separate superheater furnace; in others, the superheater tubes project into the same furnace that is used for the generation of saturated steam.

Some question may arise concerning the need for both saturated steam and superheated steam. Saturated steam is used for operating most steam-driven auxiliary machinery; reciprocating machinery, in particular, requires saturated steam for the lubrication of the moving parts of the steam end. Superheated steam is used almost exclusively for the propulsion turbines. There is more available energy in superheated steam than in saturated steam at the same pressure; and the use of higher temperatures vastly increases the efficiency of the propulsion cycle since, as we have seen, the efficiency of a heat engine is dependent upon the absolute temperature at the source (boiler) and the absolute temperature at the receiver (condenser). In some instances, the gain in efficiency resulting from the use of superheated steam may be as much as 15 percent for 200 degrees of superheat. This increase in efficiency is particularly important because it allows substantial savings in fuel consumption and in space and weight requirements. A further advantage in using superheated steam for propulsion machinery is that it causes relatively little erosion since it is free of moisture

II. CLASSIFICATION

Boilers may be classified in a number of different ways, according to various design features. Most commonly, they are classified and described in terms of (1) the relative location of the fire and water spaces, (2) the size of the tubes, (3) the type of circulation, and (4) the type of superheat. Some knowledge of these methods of classification will be useful in understanding the design and construction of modern boilers.

A. Location of Fire and Water Spaces

First of all, boilers are classified according to the relative location of their fire and water spaces. By this classification, all boilers may be divided into two groups: *fire-tube boilers* and *water-tube boilers*. In *fire-tube boilers*, the gases of combustion flow through the tubes and thereby heat the surrounding water. In *water-tube boilers*, the water flows through the tubes and is heated by the gases of combustion that fill the furnace.

B. Size of Tubes

Water-tube boilers are further classified according to the size of the tubes. Boilers having tubes 2 inches or more in diameter are called *large-tube boilers*. Boilers having tubes less than 2 inches in diameter are called *small-tube* or *express-type boilers*.

C. Type of Circulation

Water-tube boilers are also classified as *natural circulation boilers* or as *force circulation boilers*, depending upon the way in which the water circulates within the boiler.

Natural circulation boilers are those in which the circulation of water depends upon the difference in density between an ascending mixture of hot water and steam and a descending body of relatively cool and steam-free water. Natural circulation may be of two types, free or accelerated.

In this type of boiler, the generating tubes are installed at a slight angle of inclination which allows the lighter hot water and steam to rise while the cooler (and heavier) water descends.

Installing the generating tubes at a greater angle of inclination increases the rate of water circulation. Hence, boilers in which the tubes slope more steeply are said to have accelerated natural circulation.

Most modern boilers are designed for accelerated natural circulation. In such boilers, large tubes (3 or more inches in diameter) are installed between the steam drum and the water drums. These tubes, called *downcomers*, are located outside the furnace and away from the heat of combustion, thereby serving as pathways for the downward flow of relatively cool water. When a sufficient number of downcomers are installed, all small tubes can be generating tubes, carrying steam and water upward; and all downward flow can be carried by the downcomer. The size and number of downcomers installed varies from one type of boiler to another.

Forced circulation boilers are, as their name implies, quite different in design from the boilers that utilize natural circulation. Instead of depending upon differences in density between the hotter and the cooler water, forced circulation boilers use pumps to force the water through the various boiler circuits. Forced circulation boilers are relatively new, but they have some very definite advantages which will probably lead to their increased use in the future.

D. Type of Superheat

Practically all boilers are equipped with superheaters. With respect to the superheater installation, boilers are classified as having either controlled superheat or uncontrolled superheat. In a boiler with *controlled superheat*, the degree of superheat can be changed by regulating the amount of heat supplied to the superheater tube bank, without substantially changing the amount of heat supplied to the generating tubes. This control of superheat is possible because the boiler has two furnaces, one for the saturated side and one for the superheat side. A boiler with *uncontrolled superheat*, on the other hand, has only one furnace; and since the same furnace must be used for heating both the generating tubes and the superheater tubes, the degree of superheat cannot be controlled but varies within a small range as a function of design and firing rate.

Various terms are used to describe these two basic types of superheaters. Where the superheat is controlled, the superheater is often referred to as an *integral, separately fired superheat*, and the boiler as a whole is called a *superheat control boiler*. Where the superheat is not controlled, the superheater may be called an *integral, not separately fired superheater*, or it may be referred to as a *no control,* or *uncontrolled superheater*, and the boiler as a whole is called a *no control* or *uncontrolled superheat boiler*. The term *integral* is used to indicate that the superheater is installed as a part of the boiler unit. Practically all superheaters on modern boilers are integral with the boilers.

On both controlled and uncontrolled superheat boilers, the superheater tubes are protected from radiant heat by generation tubes that are called *water screen tubes.* The water screen tubes absorb the intense radiant heat of the furnace, and the superheater tubes are heated by convection currents rather than by direct radiation. Hence, the superheaters are sometimes called *convection-type superheaters.*

Some older types of superheat control boilers had *radiant-type superheaters*—that is, the superheater tubes were not screened by water tubes but were exposed directly to the radiant heat of the furnace. However, this type of superheater is relatively uncommon at the present time and will, therefore, not be further discussed.

III. TERMINOLOGY

In order to ensure uniform use of terms, there has been established a number of standard terms and definitions pertaining to boilers. Some of the more important of these definitions are given below.

A. Fire Room and Boiler Room: A compartment which contains boilers and the station for operating them is called a *fire room*. A compartment which contains boilers which does not contain the station for operating them is called a *boiler room*.

B. Boiler Emergency Station: This term is used to designate a station which is so located that, in the event of trouble, one may proceed with minimum delay to any fire room, boiler operating station, or boiler room.

C. Boiler Full-Power Capacity: The total quantity of steam required to develop contract shaft horsepower of the vessel, divided by the number of boilers installed, gives boiler full-power capacity. The quantity of steam is given in pounds of water evaporated per hour. Full-power capacity is indicated in the manufacturer's technical manual for each boiler.

D. Boiler Overload Capacity: Boiler overload capacity is specified in the design of the boiler. It is given in terms of steaming rate or firing rate, depending upon the individual installation. Boiler overload capacity is usually 120 percent of boiler full-power capacity.

E. Superheater Outlet Pressure: This is the actual steam pressure at the superheater outlet.

F. Steam Drum Pressure: This is the pressure in the steam drum. Steam drum pressure is specified in the design of a boiler and is given in the manufacturer's technical manual for each boiler. Steam drum pressure is the pressure which must be carried in the boiler steam drum in order to obtain the required pressure at the turbine throttles, when steaming at full-power capacity. Ordinarily, the designed steam drum pressure is carried for all steaming conditions.

G. Design Pressure: Design pressure is the pressure specified by the boiler manufacturer as a criterion for boiler design. It is usually 103 percent of steam drum pressure.

H. Operating Pressure: Operating pressure is the pressure at the final outlet from a boiler, after steam has passed through all baffles, the dry pipe, the superheater, etc., when the boiler is steaming at full-power capacity. Operating pressure is specified in the design of a boiler and is given in the manufacturer's technical manual. Operating pressure is the same as superheater outlet pressure when the boiler is steaming at full-power capacity; when the boiler is steaming at less than full-power capacity, however, the actual pressure at the superheater outlet will vary from the specified operating pressure provided a constant drum pressure is maintained.

I. Boiler Efficiency: The efficiency of a boiler is the British thermal units per pound of fuel absorbed by the water and steam divided by the British thermal units per pound of fuel fired. In other words, boiler efficiency is output divided by input, or Btu utilized divided by Btu available. Boiler efficiency is expressed as a percentage.

J. Fire Room Efficiency: The boiler efficiency corrected for blower and pump steam consumption is known as fire room efficiency. (This is not the same as boiler plant efficiency or propulsion plant efficiency.)

K. Total Heating Surface: The total heating surface of any steam generating unit consists of that portion of the heat transfer apparatus which is exposed on one side to the gases of combustion and on the other side to the water or steam being heated. Thus, the total heating surface equals the sum of the generating surface, the superheater surface, and the economizer surface. All heating surfaces are measured on the combustion-gas side.

L. Generating Surface: The generating surface is that portion of the total heating surface in which the fluid being heated forms part of the circulating system. The generating surface includes the boiler tube banks, water walls, water screens, and water floors (where installed and not covered by refractory material.)

M. Superheater Surface: The superheater surface is that portion of the total heating surface where the steam is heated after leaving the boiler steam drum.

N. Economizer Surface: The economizer surface is that portion of the total heating surface where the feed water is heated before entering the generating system.

O. Steaming Hours: The term steaming hours includes the time during which the boiler has fires lighted for raising steam and the time during which it is generating steam. Time during which fires are not lighted is not included in steaming hours.

GLOSSARY OF BOILER TERMS

CONTENTS

	Page
Atomize ...... Condensate	1
Damper ...... Gravity (specific)	2
Heaters ...... Modulation	3
Oil Pressure ...... Pulsating	4
Ratio ...... Smoke Alarm	5
Solvent ...... Windbox	6

GLOSSARY OF BOILER TERMS

A

ATOMIZE To break into tiny bits or mist.

ATOMIZING CUP Cone in the burner assembly which spins the oil into a mist for burning.

B

BOILER FIRETUBES Tubes through which the heat from the furnace flows to heat the water in the boiler.

BREECHING Connection (channel or pipe) from boiler to stack.

BTU British Thermo Unit; the amount of heat necessary to raise the temperature of 1 lb. of water 1 F at or near maximum density.

BURNER COVER Cover which should be used over burner opening when burner is swung out (venturi cover). Failure to cover opening might cause refractory to be damaged from cold air shock.

BURNER CUP Atomizing cup; cup which spins the oil into a fine mist for burning.

BURNER HING Joint(s) on which the burner can be swung away from the main boiler assembly.

BURNER MOTOR Motor providing the power to spin the atomizing cup.

C

CHECK VALVES A valve permitting oil to flow in one direction only; used to prevent oil from returning to the tank when the pump shuts down

CIRCUIT BREAKER Device for the automatic interruption of an electrical circuit when a problem occurs.

COMBUSTION Burning; the interaction of oil with oxygen in air accompanied by a well defined flame releasing heat.

CONDENDATE Water formed by cooling steam.

D

DAMPER — Device which checks or regulates the draft (air) flow.

DIAPHRAGM — Fiat disk of metal or rubber which bends in response to pressure changes.

DIPSTICK — Long stick used to measure the depth of a liquid.

DRAFT — Air flow caused by chimney effect or by a blower (fan).

DRAFT CONTROLS — Ways of regulating the air flow.

E

EMISSION — Undesirable combustion products such as smoke, soot, SO_2 etc.

F

FAN CASING — The fan cover which permits access to the fan.

FIREBOX — The furnace; where combustion takes place.

FLAME ROD — Sensor inserted in the flame to establish and monitor proper ignition.

FLAME SCANNER — Sensor to establish or monitor proper ignition based on presence of ultra-violet rays; purple peeper.

FLASH POINT — Temperature (determined by laboratory test) which indicates the fire safety of the fuel.

FLUE GAS — Products of burning fuel.

FLUE GAS TEMPERATURE — Temperature of gases as they leave the boiler.

FUEL NOZZLE — Fitting at the end of the oil supply line which distributes the oil into the cup.

G

GRAVITY (specific) — The comparison of the ratio of the weight of a gallon of oil to a gallon of water; measured in degrees API (American Petroleum Institute); low gravity indicates heavy oil.

H

HEATERS Equipment which raises the oil to the required tern perature for pumping, flow, and burning; boiler systems are equipped with an electric heater and a steam or hot water oil heater.

I

IGNITION The act of lighting fuel; light-off.

IMPINGEMENT When flame touches refractories so as to impair combustion.

J

JUMPER Means for cutting an electrical control out of the circuit.

L

LATCH-OUT SWITCH Safety switch; device which protects the boiler by shutting down the system in the event of flame failure.

LOUVERS Movable, multiple panels for controlling air flow.

LOW WATER CUT-OFF Automatically shuts off the burner when the water in the boiler is too low.

M

MAGNETIC OIL VALVE Control which starts and stops oil from entering the atomizing cup.

MASTER CONTROLLER (programmer. Projector Relay) Device on the main panel board which starts and stops the burner safely.

METERING VALVE Automatic oil flow valve connected to the Primary and Secondary air dampers so that burner operation can be modulated.

MODULATING MOTOR Motor that drives the linkages to oil and air valves.
MODULATION Automatic matching of the burner oil input with the correct air flow to meet the heating demands of the building.

O

OIL PRESSURE — The force required to move the oil.

OIL PRESSURE GAUGE Instrument used to measure oil pressure.

OIL TEMPERATURE INTERLOCK — Thermostatic control set to prevent the burner from operating until the oil reaches the proper viscosity for good combustion.

OIL TRANSFER PUMP Motor driven pump providing the pressure required to move oil from the tank to the burner.

P

PARTICULATES — Any solid or liquid (other than water) which is so small as to be capable of being carried by the wind or suspended in air.

PHOTO CELL — The sensor which proves the presence of a flame, thus insuring a safe light-off.

PILOT — A gas burner used to light the main oil burner.

POST-PURGE — Continuing burner fan operation after the flame is shut off in order to clean any residual oil or gas vapors remaining in the boiler.

POUR POINT — Measure of the effect of temperature on the ability of oil to flow; is measured by cooling the oil until it just moves.

PRE-PURGE — Burner fan operation before ignition to insure absence of combustion vapors in the boiler.

PRESSURE RELIEF VALVE — Valve set at a pressure to permit the oil to return to the tank when not needed to meet the burner need.

PRIMARY AIR SHUTTER — Adjustable, automatic means of controlling the primary air to the burner.

PSI — Pounds per Square Inch a unit of pressure.

PULSATING — Rhythmic changing of the flame shape.

R

RATIO — The relation of one substance to another; in boilers the relation of the right amount of air to the right amount of oil is the proper air/oil ratio.

REFRACTORY — Special brick lining for the firebox in the boiler.

RELAY — Part of control system used to transfer electrical impulses.

RESET — Generally refers to the main overriding safety control valve; must be manually turned back on in the event of automatic shutdown.

RESIDUAL — Refinery term for the end product of oil processing; descriptive word for # 6 oil.

RINGELMANN CHART — Chart used to measure the severity of air pollution by how dark the smoke is.

ROTARY CUP — Polished brass cone in burner which spins to atomize the oil.

S

SAFETY CONTROL SENSORS — Parts of the safety system located in the firebox and used to prove the existence of flames.

SCHEMATIC DIAGRAM — A diagram drawn to show the proper order and relation of things rather than how they actually look.

SECONDARY AIR — Air supply around the burner flame from the windbox.

SECONDARY AIR DAMPER — Damper on the windbox usually in the form of louvers to control secondary air flow.

SEDEMENT — Undesirable residues in oil.

SEQUENTIAL DRAFT CONTROLLER — A regulator in the breeching which adjusts stack draft.

SMOKE ALARM — Device in the breeching which responds to smoke by setting off an alarm.

SOLVENT	Organic liquid used for cleaning; usually kerosene or Stoddard's solvent.
SPINNING CUP	The atomizing cone in the burner.
STRAINERS	Large and fine mesh sieves in the oil lines which remove residue.
SUCTION BELL	Device in the storage tank where a limited amount of oil is heated for pumping.

T

TRIAL FOR IGNITION	Time period provided to complete the ignition cycle; normally about 10 seconds. If ignition does not take place within this time, the boiler shuts down (some systems permit a second trial).

V

VACUUM GAUGE	An oil pressure gauge on the oil line (on inlet side of pump) which indicates clogging of oil line.
VISCOSITY	A measure of the ability of oil to flow.

W

WINDBOX	A louvered cover designed to permit modulation of the secondary air flow.